FRANCIS FRITH'S

LANCASHIRE
A SECOND SELECTION
PHOTOGRAPHIC MEMORIES

DENNIS and JAN KELSALL are freelance writers and photographers. In addition to their collections of countryside and hill walks, they have produced a number of detailed travel guides covering various parts of the country. They have also been occasional contributors to AA publications and magazines, and they produce a weekly walking column for the Lancashire Evening Post. They have contributed to several other volumes of the Francis Frith photographic collections. Although Dennis and Jan's work now takes them to many different places throughout the country and beyond, they continue to live in their native Lancashire where, despite a lifetime of exploration, they find they are still discovering new corners that surprise and delight.

FRANCIS FRITH'S
PHOTOGRAPHIC MEMORIES

LANCASHIRE

PHOTOGRAPHIC MEMORIES

DENNIS AND JAN KELSALL

First published in the United Kingdom in 2003 by
Frith Book Company Ltd

Hardback Edition 2003
ISBN 1-85937-455-7

British Library Cataloguing in Publication Data

Francis Frith's Lancashire - A Second Selection
Dennis and Jan Kelsall

Frith Book Company Ltd
Frith's Barn, Teffont,
Salisbury, Wiltshire SP3 5QP
Tel: +44 (0) 1722 716 376
Email: info@francisfrith.co.uk
www.francisfrith.co.uk

Printed and bound in Great Britain

Front Cover: **FLEETWOOD**, *The Beach 1892* 30421

Frontispiece: **WHALLEY**, *The Viaduct from the Nab 1901* 47060

AS WITH ANY HISTORICAL DATABASE THE FRITH ARCHIVE IS CONSTANTLY
BEING CORRECTED AND IMPROVED AND THE PUBLISHERS WOULD
WELCOME INFORMATION ON OMISSIONS OR INACCURACIES

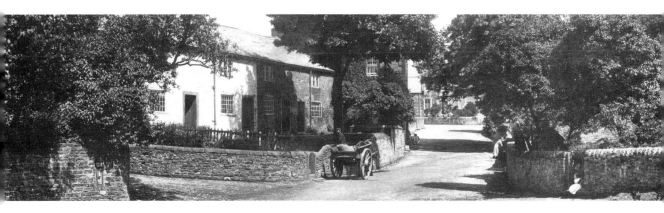

CONTENTS

FRANCIS FRITH
VICTORIAN PIONEER

FRANCIS FRITH, founder of the world-famous photographic archive, was a complex and multi-talented man. A devout Quaker and a highly successful Victorian businessman, he was philosophic by nature and pioneering in outlook.

By 1855 he had already established a wholesale grocery business in Liverpool, and sold it for the astonishing sum of £200,000, which is the equivalent today of over £15,000,000. Now a multi-millionaire, he was able to indulge his passion for travel. As a child he had pored over travel books written by early explorers, and his fancy and imagination had been stirred by family holidays to the sublime mountain regions of Wales and Scotland. 'What a land of spirit-stirring and enriching scenes and places!' he had written. He was to return to these scenes of grandeur in later years to 'recapture the thousands of vivid and tender memories', but with a different purpose. Now in his thirties, and captivated by the new science of photography, Frith set out on a series of pioneering journeys up the Nile and to the Near East that occupied him from 1856 until 1860.

INTRIGUE AND EXPLORATION

These far-flung journeys were packed with intrigue and adventure. In his life story, written when he was sixty-three, Frith tells of being held captive by bandits, and of fighting 'an awful midnight battle to the very point of surrender with a deadly pack of hungry, wild dogs'. Wearing flowing Arab costume, Frith arrived at Akaba by camel seventy years before Lawrence of Arabia, where he encountered 'desert princes and rival sheikhs, blazing with jewel-hilted swords'.

He was the first photographer to venture beyond the sixth cataract of the Nile. Africa was still the mysterious 'Dark Continent', and Stanley and Livingstone's historic meeting was a decade into the future. The conditions for picture taking confound belief. He laboured for hours in his wicker dark-room in the sweltering heat of the desert, while the volatile chemicals fizzed dangerously in their trays. Back in London he exhibited his photographs and was 'rapturously cheered' by members of the Royal Society. His reputation as a photographer was made overnight.

VENTURE OF A LIFE-TIME

Characteristically, Frith quickly spotted the opportunity to create a new business as a specialist publisher of photographs. He lived in an era of immense and sometimes violent change.

For the poor in the early part of Victoria's reign work was exhausting and the hours long, and people had precious little free time to enjoy themselves. Most had no transport other than a cart or gig at their disposal, and rarely travelled far beyond the boundaries of their own town or village. However, by the 1870s the railways had threaded their way across the country, and Bank Holidays and half-day Saturdays had been made obligatory by Act of Parliament. All of a sudden the working man and his family were able to enjoy days out and see a little more of the world.

With typical business acumen, Francis Frith foresaw that these new tourists would enjoy having souvenirs to commemorate their days out. In 1860 he married Mary Ann Rosling and set out on a new career: his aim was to photograph every city, town and village in Britain. For the next thirty years he travelled the country by train and by pony and trap, producing fine photographs of seaside resorts and beauty spots that were keenly bought by millions of Victorians. These prints were painstakingly pasted into family albums and pored over during the dark nights of winter, rekindling precious memories of summer excursions.

THE RISE OF FRITH & CO

Frith's studio was soon supplying retail shops all over the country. To meet the demand he gath-

ered about him a small team of photographers, and published the work of independent artist-photographers of the calibre of Roger Fenton and Francis Bedford. In order to gain some understanding of the scale of Frith's business one only has to look at the catalogue issued by Frith & Co in 1886: it runs to some 670 pages, listing not only many thousands of views of the British Isles but also many photographs of most European countries, and China, Japan, the USA and Canada - note the sample page shown here from the hand-written Frith & Co ledgers recording the pictures. By 1890 Frith had created the greatest specialist photographic publishing company in the world, with over 2,000 sales outlets - more than the combined number that Boots and WH Smith have today! The picture on the nest page shows the Frith & Co display board at Ingleton in the Yorkshire Dales. Beautifully constructed with mahogany frame and gilt inserts, it could display up to a dozen local scenes.

POSTCARD BONANZA

The ever-popular holiday postcard we know today took many years to develop. In 1870 the Post Office issued the first plain cards, with a pre-printed stamp on one face. In 1894 they allowed other publishers' cards to be sent through the mail with an attached adhesive half-penny stamp. Demand grew rapidly, and in 1895 a new size of postcard was permitted called the court card, but there was little room for illustration. In 1899, a year after Frith's death, a new card measuring 5.5 x 3.5 inches became the standard format, but it was not until 1902 that the divided back came into being, so that the address and message could be on one face and a full-size illustration on the other. Frith & Co were in the vanguard of postcard development: Frith's sons Eustace and Cyril continued their father's monumental task, expanding the number of views offered to the public and recording more

and more places in Britain, as the coasts and countryside were opened up to mass travel.

Francis Frith had died in 1898 at his villa in Cannes, his great project still growing. The archive he created continued in business for another seventy years. By 1970 it contained over a third of a million pictures showing 7,000 British towns and villages.

FRANCIS FRITH'S LEGACY

Frith's legacy to us today is of immense significance and value, for the magnificent archive of evocative photographs he created provides a unique record of change in the cities, towns and villages throughout Britain over a century and more. Frith and his fellow studio photographers revisited locations many times down the years to update their views, compiling for us an enthralling and colourful pageant of British life and character.

We are fortunate that Frith was dedicated to recording the minutiae of everyday life. For it is this sheer wealth of visual data, the painstaking chronicle of changes in dress, transport, street layouts, buildings, housing, engineering and landscape that captivates us so much today. His remarkable images offer us a powerful link with the past and with the lives of our ancestors.

THE VALUE OF THE ARCHIVE TODAY

Computers have now made it possible for Frith's many thousands of images to be accessed almost instantly. Frith's images are increasingly used as visual resources, by social historians, by researchers into genealogy and ancestry, by architects and town planners, and by teachers involved in local history projects.

In addition, the archive offers every one of us an opportunity to examine the places where we and our families have lived and worked down the years. Highly successful in Frith's own era, the archive is now, a century and more on, entering a new phase of popularity. Historians consider the Francis Frith Collection to be of prime national importance. It is the only archive of its kind remaining in private ownership. Francis Frith's archive is now housed in an historic timber barn in the beautiful village of Teffont in Wiltshire. Its founder would not recognize the archive office as it is today. In place of the many thousands of dusty boxes containing glass plate negatives and an all-pervading odour of photographic chemicals, there are now ranks of computer screens. He would be amazed to watch his images travelling round the world at unimaginable speeds through internet lines.

The archive's future is both bright and exciting. Francis Frith, with his unshakeable belief in making photographs available to the greatest number of people, would undoubtedly approve of what is being done today with his lifetime's work. His photographs depicting our shared past are now bringing pleasure and enlightenment to millions around the world a century and more after his death.

LANCASHIRE
AN INTRODUCTION

IF YOU'VE NEVER been to Lancashire, you might be forgiven for accepting the 'cloth cap and clogs' image portrayed by so many seaside post cards, films and television soaps. True, that was what people wore, and some still do if you know where to look, yet the same could equally be said of many other areas in the country where the Victorian industrial revolution took hold, for cloth caps and clogs were often all that the ordinary working man could afford.

However, as you will discover from these photographs, this is only one image from a richly varied county, whose features and qualities compare with some of the country's finest, whether it be the countryside's natural beauty, bold and exiting architecture, plain honest-to-goodness entertainment or accomplished art in many fields.

The border that separates Lancashire from its neighbours traces a meandering line that, for the

STONYHURST, *The College 1899* 43487

most part, lies across windswept, lonely hills and vast, open moors. Before 1974, the county stretched from the Three Counties Stone at the top of the Wrynose Pass, now in Cumbria, down to the River Mersey, south of Manchester. That Westmorland apparently isolated Furness from the rest of Lancashire was not an anomaly, since the two had been linked since antiquity by the vast expanse of sand revealed each time the tide retreated from Morecambe Bay. It was not until the middle of the 19th century, when a railway was laid across the marshy estuaries of the Kent and Leven on the back of steel-piled viaducts, that there was a practical alternative to the direct, if hazardous, crossing. Today, the county is much reduced, 'Lancashire across the sands' and much of the large conurbations of Merseyside and Manchester have been lost, and the border with its long-standing rival, Yorkshire, has been redrawn, although neither county is really sure who got the better of the deal. But for many, these changes are merely administrative meddlings and their traditional allegiances remain unchanged. Lancashire is, as it always was, the area covered within this book.

Within the county is huge diversity in the shape and character of the land. Behind much of the coast and in the area between Manchester and Warrington, are expansive, low-lying plains. Once largely marsh and wind-blown sand, drainage and reclamation schemes over the centuries have won from them some of the country's richest agricultural land and created space for 'new' towns, particularly along the coast, where several seaside holiday resorts sprang up in the mid-19th century. To the east, the ground rises to the Pennines, that great chain of hilly moorland known as the 'backbone of England', where lies some of the county's most isolated hamlets and farmsteads. Yet it was from those hills

that much of Lancashire's early wealth derived, off the backs of the countless sheep that grazed the lonely uplands. Those same hills spawned the first industrial age, when the powerful, fast flowing streams coursing through the valleys were harnessed to drive machinery in textile mills, initially producing woollen cloth before switching to cotton, to which the damp, cool climate is so admirably suited. The wooded hills and valleys of Furness, too, were once equally industrialised, producing iron and gunpowder as well as a host of wooden articles, notably millions of bobbins for the Pennine mills.

The construction of the canals and the development of the steam engine, however, closed many of the early factories. Previously, the only economically effective means of transporting heavy or bulky goods had been by boat. Whilst packhorse trains and lumbering carts could just about cope with the small water-powered factories, there was no way that they could handle the production capacity offered by steam power, particularly if that meant bringing in the coal as well. As a result, industry shifted to the coalfields of central and eastern Lancashire and to those places served by the growing network of canals and navigable waterways. Further development sprang up beside the railways that followed a century later, but in the main, the die had already been cast and the great industrial areas of the 1950s were those that had been born in the boom at the end of the 18th century. Wander now through the valleys around Rusland and Backbarrow, or along the Pennine slopes where the canals never reached, and it is hard to imagine them as the thriving industrial centres they once were. Nature has reclaimed its own, smoothing over the scars of old factories and workings to create a very different and often intriguing landscape.

It was the wealth generated by the region's factories and businesses that built the imposing, architectural masterpieces and cultural institutions that now grace many of its towns and cities. In many instances, the industrialists and entrepreneurs gave much back to the places where they made their money; raising impressive municipal and commercial buildings in the town centres and providing facilities for the education, recreation and cultural development of the people who toiled in their factories. Many of Lancashire's fine churches, schools, hospitals, libraries, museums and art galleries were founded and often substantially paid for by these self-made men. Of course, the gestures were not necessarily always philanthropic, for a town that looked grand and prosperous was better placed to attract new trade and commerce. But, whatever their motivation, they have left behind a rich heritage of Victorian architecture hardly surpassed anywhere else in the country.

Those same industries were also the raison d'être behind the boom of the coastal holiday resorts. The 18th century had seen the popularisation of sea-cures and therapies amongst the middle and upper classes, which soon developed into a wider recreational context, but until the railway age, ordinary people had neither the time nor money to visit the seaside. However, with the prospect of speedy and relatively cheap travel, the people flocked there in their thousands and so began the tradition of an annual break from the toil and drudgery of the factories. Resorts competed to attract customers, building ever more impressive promenades, piers, pavilions, theatres and other places of entertainment, a race that culminated in the construction of the famous Blackpool Tower, which, from the day it opened, has been a universally popular attraction.

LIVERPOOL, *Dale Street 1887* 20002

The majority of these photographs were taken during the closing years of the 19th century and the first decades of the 20th century, a period of rapid and momentous change that affected almost every facet of the country's way of life. The agricultural, industrial and transport revolutions of the past had irrevocably altered the structure of society, moving people from the countryside into towns and replacing a mixed cottage economy with that of factory mass production, but the events during this time were to have at least as great an effect. The latter part of the 19th century saw the British Empire at its peak, a domain on which the sun never set. But with a new century came the dawn of a new era. War in Europe, which quickly involved most of the world, left behind it a very different order, where the old values of aristocratic rule would no longer be tolerated. Political emancipation and improving education gave ordinary people both the knowledge and confidence to demand a say in their future and have the opportunity to enjoy something of the fruits of their labours.

In this collection of pictures, we can see some of these transformations taking place. The formal social proprieties and distinctions of the Victorians rapidly gave way to a more uniform and relaxed society, and a mechanised, consumer-orientated way of life steadily displaced the frugality of make-do-and-mend. All aspects of life were affected by these changes and people began to move about the country to an extent never before imagined. Electric trams and then motorised buses replaced horse-drawn carts and omnibuses in the towns, whilst increasing car ownership gave ordinary folk the freedom to go where and when they pleased, allowing families to enjoy a day-out by the sea or take

LYTHAM, *Lifeboat House 1907* 59125

a picnic into the countryside, something almost unheard of a generation earlier. Shops too changed, look at the earlier photographs and you will see that every town street is different. Small stores run by local families were the order of the day, with many selling just about everything you could want under one roof. Today's high streets are a very different place, dominated by huge retail outlets whose capacity to buy in bulk has forced many of the independent shopkeepers out of business. Yet, in some things we have probably lost more than we have gained, for the old shopkeepers knew their trade and strove to please, since if they didn't, they knew that customers would go elsewhere.

In wandering around the county identifying some of these pictures, we spoke to many people, and often a simple question would generate an hour-long conversation as they recounted what 'used to be' and how things have changed. Time quickly flew by, their stories more interesting than any found in history books. One thing on which there was almost universal agreement is that the scenes portrayed in the photographs invariably present a more attractive picture than does the same view today. Few people had much to say that was complimentary about modern buildings and developments and deplored the proliferation of banal advertising, street clutter and rubbish that has invaded our towns.

GLASSON, *The Docks c1955* G260012

But not all that is new is bad, and there will be some of today's buildings and structures that will stand the test of time and cause future generations to stop and ponder. It is also true that we tend to look back at 'what was' through 'rose-tinted spectacles', and nostalgia often taints our perceptions. But few of these pictures show the less desirable face of late Victorian towns, the acres of close-packed, back to back hovels that housed the majority of ordinary people, nor do they illustrate the drudgery and hardship of the working lives the majority endured. There can not be many people who would want to revert to the pre-Beveridge days, despite the short-comings of today's systems. But it is not only the towns and cities that have been captured here, these photographs also depict many of Lancashire's picturesque villages and the countryside that surrounds them, where sometimes, there appears to have been surprisingly little change.

Although the past can never be recreated, these old photographs have often captured something of the spirit and mood of their time and have the power to stir our memories and imaginations. Turn the pages and enjoy a trip back through the years to the Lancashire of an earlier century.

BURNLEY, *Ormerod Hall 1895* 35805

THE INDUSTRIAL SOUTH & EAST

ECCLES
Church Street c1960 E88016

Many of these buildings have been demolished to make way for retail development and road alterations, whilst the Broadway Cinema out-lived its silver screen only to end its days as a supermarket. Further along the road is the main post office and at the end, distinguished by its clock tower, is the Town Hall, which was built in 1880.

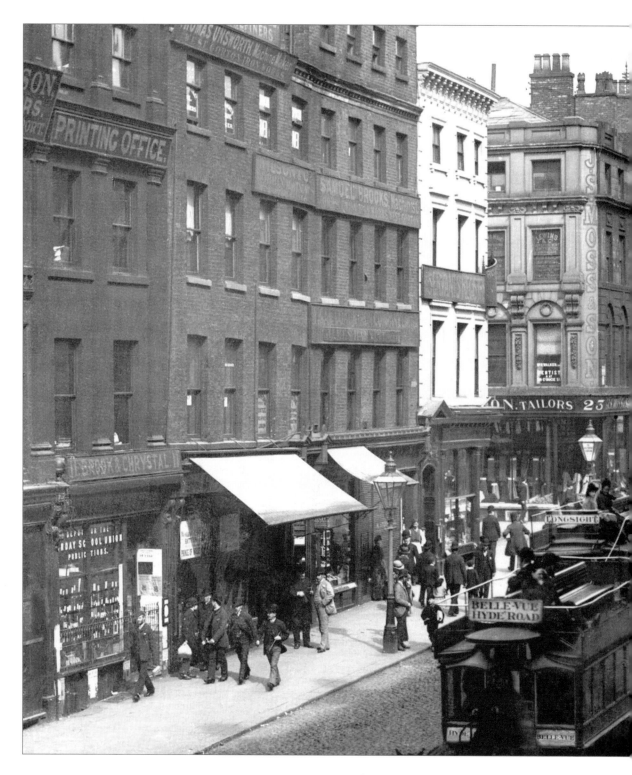

MANCHESTER
Market Street 1889
21899

Late 19th-century Market Street is lined by a miscellany of individualistic shops, a far cry from the predictable monotony of today's high street outlets. Then, as now, trams were a mainstay of the city's transport, but pulled by horses like the omnibuses and carts that also line the street, whilst hatted business men with canes and shoppers walk the pavements.

► **MANCHESTER**
*St Ann's Square
1885* 18263

St Ann's Square, named after its lovely early 18th-century church, once overlooked green fields, but within a century had been absorbed within the city's commercial heart. The Royal Exchange was founded in 1806 and amongst the waiting hackney carriages is Richard Cobden's statue. He now stands by the church, having stepped back to make room for the city's war memorial.

◄ **MIDDLETON**
*Ye Olde Boar's Head
c1955* M311502

Middleton is an ancient place, its name suggesting a Saxon origin and, with such a history, it is heartening to know that some of its very old buildings still survive. One is this 16th-century inn which stands on the corner of Long Street. Half-timbered and built upon a stone plinth, it was apparently once used as the courtroom and jail.

▲ ROCHDALE, *Town Hall Square 1892* 30396

Overspending on civic projects is not peculiar to present-day administrations, for the final bill for Rochdale's Town Hall was over 7½ times the original £20,000 estimate when it eventually opened in 1871. Behind, on top of Sparrow Hill, is St Chad's Church, which, although much renovated at the end of the 19th century, traces its history to a Saxon foundation.

◄ ROCHDALE
*Newgate
1897* 30400A

This picture is, perhaps, more representative of working-class Rochdale and shows telephone wires and electric tram cables strung like knitting above the street. Men on their way to work, one carrying a pail, stop to watch the photographer at work, and perhaps the policeman is finishing a tour of night duty, for he is clad in his uniform greatcoat.

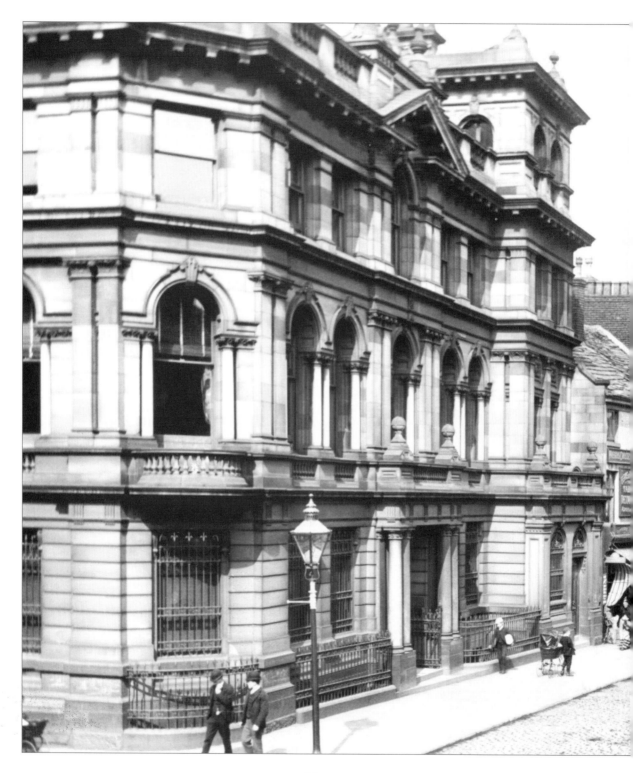

BOLTON
Deansgate 1895 35850

Ladies in long dresses and shawls and bowler-hatted gentlemen wander amongst the shops, several of which display their wares outside to attract customers.
The track along the centre of the street was for horse-drawn trams, which began operating in 1880. The service was electrified in 1900 and ran for 47 years, carrying 56 million passengers a year at its peak.

▲ **BOLTON**
Hall i'th Wood 1894 34389

Although no longer 'i'th wood' this wonderful building is still full of character. Begun in 1483 by Lawrence Brownlow, owner of a fulling-mill, it was extended by his descendants and again, after the Civil War, by Alexander Norris. In 1799 Samuel Compton developed his spinning mule here and now, a museum in the house charts the development of textile manufacture.

▶ **TURTON,** *The Tower 1897* 40104

A comfortable Tudor farmhouse beside a 15th-century pele, Turton Tower is associated with Humphrey Chetham, remembered for the free library, school and hospital that he founded in Manchester. James Kay, who lived here when the Manchester to Bolton railway was built, required the bridges on his estate to be decorated with battlemented towers, to preserve its character.

LIVERPOOL
Dale Street 1887 20002

Horse-drawn trams, hackney carriages and heavy-wheeled goods
carts rattle along the stone setts of Dale Street, passing some of
the city's major financial and commercial buildings. On the far
right are the offices of the Royal Insurance and beyond the
Temple is the Prudential Assurance Building. Further along,
crowned by a soaring clock tower, stands the imposing
Renaissance-style Municipal Building.

► **LIVERPOOL**
The Exchange
1890 26663

The now-demolished Exchange overlooks a courtyard, known as Exchange Flags, where Liverpool's merchants used to meet to conduct their business. In the centre is a monument erected in 1813 to Lord Nelson, the first public sculpture commissioned for the city. It actually served another purpose too, providing ventilation for warehouses that lay beneath the square.

◄ **WARRINGTON**
Cromwell Statue
1901 47251

Much of Lancashire was affected by the Civil Wars, and Warrington, an important crossing on the Mersey and chosen by the Royalist, Lord Derby for his headquarters, saw considerable action. The Parliamentarians first took the town in 1643 and it was again the scene of fighting during the 1648 war, when Cromwell actually stayed here, his visit remembered in this statue.

▲ **WIGAN,** *The Parish Church 1895* 36810

If any spot in Wigan lays claim to being attractive, it is perhaps the precincts of its ancient parish church that should have the honour. The earliest surviving reference to All Saints is from 1199, but the present building, although much rebuilt by the Victorians, reflects the solid architectural style of 15th-century Perpendicular Gothic.

◀ **DARWEN**
Bold Venture Park 1895
35739

Parks were an important feature in many Victorian industrial towns and served as an escape from the noise, dirt and labour of the mills and factories. This fine example, not far from the town centre, was developed out of abandoned stone quarries, and features wooded corners, floral displays and lawns, all surrounding a lake fed by a 60-foot high waterfall.

▲ **BLACKBURN,** *The Cathedral 1923* 74072

Behind Victoria, bearing the traditional symbols of her office, stands St Mary's, which was constructed a century earlier to replace a medieval building. With the formation of the Blackburn Diocese in 1926 it became the cathedral church, but proved too small for its new purpose. Subsequent alterations have incorporated it as the nave of a magnificent new building, worthy of its status.

◄ **BLACKBURN**
The Boulevard 1902
48571

Next to St Mary's is the Boulevard, once church land, but now the site of the city's bus and rail stations. The fountain replaces an ancient well, of which there were once two, and behind, on a tall pedestal, stands Gladstone. He has been moved around during the last century and now presides over the junction of Blakey Moor and Northgate.

▲ **BLACKBURN,** *Technical School 1894* 34309

A group of children sit outside the Technical School, now part of Blackburn College, but founded during Queen Victoria's Golden Jubilee celebrations. A competition produced this French Renaissance style building, which was submitted by the Manchester architects, Smith, Woodhouse and Wiloughby. The Prince of Wales laid the foundation stone in 1888 and the building eventually opened to students three years later.

◄ **BLACKBURN**
Almshouses 1895
35731

This row of quite modern-looking cottages at Bank Top, lying behind a neatly cultivated garden plot was, in fact, built in 1833. The patron was Jane Turner, whose husband had been elected in Blackburn's first parliamentary elections the previous year. The almshouses still stand and, in 1974, were given Grade 2 Listed Building status.

BLACKBURN
Pleasington Church 1894 34324

Now a Grade 1 Listed Building, work was begun on this
magnificent Catholic church, dedicated to St Mary and John the
Baptist, in 1816. The money for its construction came from John
Butler, the squire of Pleasington Hall, who was almost killed in an
accident nearby. He made the gift as a thanksgiving to God that
his life was spared.

BLACKBURN
Sudell Cross 1899 43473

The square is named after Henry Sudell, one of the town's leading 18th-century citizens. The tracks across the setts formed part of Blackburn's tramway, which opened in April 1881. Originally steam-powered, it ran all the way to nearby Darwen, and in 1899 the first section was electrified and electrification subsequently extended to Hoddlesden. Competition from buses finally brought the tramway's closure in 1949.

▼ **HASLINGDEN,** *Deardengate c1955* H456011

Now a busy road through the town, in the days before mass car ownership Deardengate was almost empty except for pedestrians. Stone setts pave the street and unobtrusive traffic lights control its junction with Manchester and Blackburn Roads. Overlooking the crossing is the Midland Bank building, recognisable from its large clock that sits above the imposing entrance.

▶ **ACCRINGTON**
Town Hall 1897 40118

Formerly the Peel Institute, the Town Hall was built in 1858 as a tribute to Sir Robert Peel. He achieved many things, but is best remembered for the formation of the Metropolitan Police and his part in repealing the hated Corn Laws, which inflated the price of bread and was, in effect, a tax upon the poor.

◄ACCRINGTON
Market Hall c1965
A19021

A decade after the Peel Institute was completed, the adjacent Market Hall was opened as the focus of the town's trade. The extravagant carving and statuary above its imposing entrance is a bold proclamation of the prosperity that 19th-century commerce and industry had brought to the town.

► ACCRINGTON
Technical School 1899 43498

Henry Hills was the first headmaster of Accrington's co-educational technical school, which opened on 28 August 1895. Built from the bricks for which the town is famous, it cost £13,000, of which the Corporation borrowed £10,000. It became the Grammar School in 1921, but was demolished in 1998 and the site developed for housing.

▲ STANHILL
The Post Office c1960 S814003

A bronze plaque on the wall commemorates James Hargreaves, who, in 1764, invented his revolutionary 'Spinning Jenny' while living here. He also invented a carding machine to untangle the fibres prior to spinning. However, harassed by rioting Luddites who saw their livelihoods threatened by the new machinery, he moved to Nottingham in 1768 as did Arkwright of Preston.

► CLAYTON-LE-MOORS
All Saints Church interior 1897
40136

The 19th-century cotton industry brought great wealth to Clayton, some of which went to build the church. It has one of the finest Victorian interiors in the area and contains some exquisitely carved marble. Shown here is the font, carried on the heads of four angels, who each bear a medallion; the one on the left depicting ears of wheat.

CLAYTON-LE-MOORS
Dunkenhalgh 1897
40140

This grand manor house, now a hotel, was built during the Elizabethan period, but was considerably extended by its Victorian occupants. For a long time even Lancashire was not safe from bands of Scottish raiding parties, and 'Dunkenhalgh' is said to derive from the name of one of the brigands who settled in the area.

BURNLEY, *Town Hall 1895* 35786

Standing beside a bridge across the River Brun, from which the town takes its name, is Burnley Town Hall. It was opened in October 1888, just thirty-three years after the Mechanics Institute, which stands next door. Built of Yorkshire stone, its pillared balconies and balustrades are an imposing sight, befitting the town's claim to the 'Capital of the Pennines'.

◀ **BURNLEY**
Gawthorpe Hall 1895
35817

Lancashire landowners since the 15th century, the family achieved prominence in 1589 when Richard Shuttleworth, a successful London lawyer, was knighted and appointed Chief Justice of Chester. His brother Lawrence, a Warwickshire rector, inherited the estate, building Gawthorpe Hall in about 1600. It was subsequently remodelled by Charles Barry, architect of the Palace of Westminster, in the 1840s.

◀ **BURNLEY**
Brunswick Chapel 1895
35800a

19th-century Wesleyans were very much pro-establishment and named many new chapels 'Brunswick' after the German Duchy which was connected with the Hanoverians, from whom Victoria was descended. The one here was completed in 1869 at a cost of nearly £14,000. It could seat up to 1,750 people and replaced a smaller chapel in Hammerton Street, which was sold to the Baptists.

▲ **BURNLEY,** *Towneley Hall 1895* 35814

It is thought that a 13th-century wooden building preceded the present hall, which was built around 1350 and, until 1902, was the home of the Towneley family. Shown here from the side, the original medieval great hall has been much altered over the centuries, the mock-Tudor mullioned windows and battlemented turrets being the most recent change.

◀ **BURNLEY**
The Kitchen, Towneley Hall c1955
B251013

The hall is now Burnley's museum and art gallery, and a fine collection it has too. Some rooms are furnished to reflect different historical periods, with the kitchen depicting the Victorian era. Huge joints or even whole animals were roasted on the spit before the fire, whilst fowl or smaller pieces would be hung from the rotating hooks.

▲ **BURNLEY,** *Hurstwood (Spencer's House) 1895* 35807

Although born in London, the Elizabethan poet Edmund Spencer was related to a Lancashire family and is believed to have spent time with them here in this house. His un-returned love for Rose Dyneley, a relative of the Towneleys, inspired his poem the Faerie Queen, but in dedicating it instead to his queen, Elizabeth, was he hopeful or just patriotic?

◄**BURNLEY**
Barcroft Hall 1895
35811

On the hillside, ¾ mile east of Towneley is this splendid house. Over the main doorway, concealed by the garden wall, the owner's name, William Barcroft, and the date 1614 is inscribed. It was built at the time of his wedding to Susan, and one of their presents, a huge table bearing their initials and dated 1613, now stands in Towneley Hall.

▲ BURNLEY
Ormerod Hall 1895 35805

Sadly, this magnificent hall no longer stands, at least on the hillside above Burnley. By the 1940s, mining subsidence had left the structure dangerous and it was dismantled and subsequently taken to America. Notice the archway to the right, it is almost identical to that at nearby Barcroft and probably the work of the same mason.

◄ COLNE
Wycoller, The Pack Horse Bridge c1960 C600022

The mechanisation of weaving in the early 19th century robbed the village of both its industry and population, and the hall, the inspiration for Ferndean Manor in Charlotte Brontë's novel Jane Eyre, was abandoned in 1818. This 13th-century packhorse bridge is one of seven crossings near the village spanning Wycoller Beck, with older clapper and clam bridges lying just upstream.

THE WEST LANCASHIRE PLAIN & ITS COAST

CROSTON, *Town Bridge c1955* C474009

A 17th-century packhorse bridge spans the River Yarrow, and beyond the cottages rises the square, battlemented tower of St Michael and All Angels' Church. Although few village buildings pre-date the 17th century, Croston is an ancient place. Tradition holds that St Aidan preached here in 651 and erected a cross, from which its name derives, 'the place of the cross'.

BURSCOUGH BRIDGE
The Village c1950
B590007

The main A59 road from Liverpool to Preston runs through the centre of the village, and at the far end, rises over the Leeds and Liverpool Canal. The waterway arrived in 1755, encouraging rapid expansion and the establishment of new industries. A second boost came 100 years later when the railway was built. Its bridge lies just behind the photographer.

ORMSKIRK, *The Church From The South West 1894* 34140

Looking more like two churches than one, Ormskirk's parish church is unique in the north for having both a tower and spire. Despite Henry VIII's break with Rome, much of Lancashire remained staunchly Catholic and stones from the dismantled Augustinian priory at Burscough were used to add the tower in which the bells that once called the monks to prayer were hung.

▲ **ORMSKIRK,** *The Park 1895* 36824

By the 18th century, Ormskirk was already an important agricultural and market town, but with the arrival of the railway in 1849 it rapidly developed as an attractive residential area for Liverpool's prosperous businessmen. With the new houses came the park, a place for gentle exercise or relaxation and a favourite walk for nannies and their prams.

◄**SCARISBRICK**
The Hall From The Lake 1896 37436

The first of the Scarisbricks was in fact Gilbert de Grubhead. He acquired the estate from his brother in the 12th century and changed his name to that by which the manor was already known. In the 1860s, Charles Scarisbrick commissioned Pugin to rebuild the ancient hall, with the soaring 100-foot tower being added after his death by his sister, Anne.

▲ **SOUTHPORT**
Lord Street 1900 46255

Lord Street was laid out in the 1820s, the buildings along it displaying a wonderful medley of architectural styles, but apart from stone setts and tram lines, its general appearance has, perhaps, changed little with the passing years. Here, a horse-cart loaded with barrels and bales makes a delivery to an ironmonger's shop, whilst a boy leans against a hand-cart.

SOUTHPORT
The Pier 1902 48582

Southport has the country's longest pleasure pier, which runs for 1,211 yards over the marine boating lake and sands to the sea with attractions that included shows and amusement arcades, as well as a miniature railway. Any similarity it might have with the railway viaduct across Morecambe Bay is no accident, for the same engineer, J Brunlees, built them both.

AROUND PRESTON & THE RIBBLE'S TRIBUTARIES'

PRESTON
Fishergate 1903 50068

The town's main commercial institutions and shops occupied many of the elegant three-storey buildings along Fishergate. At the far end of the street, the impressive church-like building is actually the Town Hall, designed in the Gothic style by Sir George Gilbert Scott and completed in 1867. However, it no longer stands, having been demolished following a fire in 1947.

◄ PRESTON
Public Library And Museum 1893 33087

The grandest monument to Harris' memory is the magnificent Public Library, Museum and Art Gallery, photographed here as it nears completion. Workmen are still busy on ladders, putting the finishing touches to the building, whilst blinds have not yet been installed at the numerous windows which pierce its ornate façade. The books and fine collection of art exhibits have yet to arrive.

◄**PRESTON**
*Harris Institute
1903* 50071

The solicitor, Edmund Harris was one of Preston's greatest benefactors, who on his death left a bequest of over £400,000 to the town. One of the buildings to carry his name is the Institute, built in the classical-revival style. Sweeping balustrades line steps up to a grand entrance portico, its pediment carried above pilasters and fluted Corinthian columns.

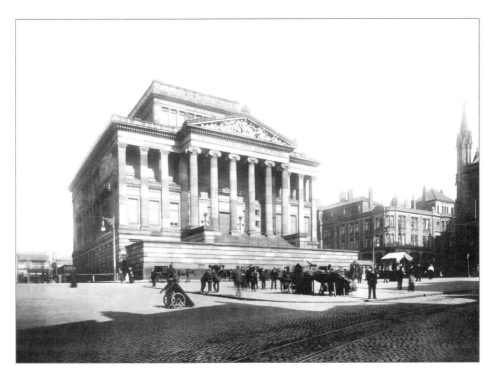

▲ **PRESTON,** *Public Library And Museum 1903* 50083

A local architect, James Hibbert designed the building, which is a monumental interpretation of the classical style, the relief above the portico depicting figures of the Greek philosophers and teachers. A market place and butchers' shambles had previously occupied the site, and traders continued to put up their stalls in the open space below the entrance.

◄**PRESTON**
New Post Office 1903
50085

Not far from the Harris Gallery is the new Head Post Office, shown here in the year that it first opened for business. Built in a very different style, it is interesting to note that the windows encircling the building have a different design on each floor. Its ornate façade is, however, hardly matched by the plain functionality of its interior.

▶ **PRESTON**
War Memorial
1926 79111

In this later photograph, Preston's war memorial now occupies the open space in front of the Post Office. The monument had only recently been unveiled and was designed by Sir Giles Gilbert Scott, who was also responsible for Whitehall's Cenotaph. Behind the two buses stands the County Sessions House, its splendid multi-columned tower rising over 170 feet into the air.

◀ **PRESTON**
Harris Orphanage
1893 33099

Another worthy establishment funded by Edwin Harris' generous bequest was this orphanage. Built on land that was purchased for £4,800, it was designed by the architect Benjamin Sykes in the 'domestic Gothic' style. The building no longer serves its original purpose, and Central Lancashire University now uses it as a conference centre.

▲ **PRESTON,** *The Railcross School For The Deaf 1897* 40997

A lawnmower stands in the corner of tennis courts, overlooked by the Railcross School for the Deaf. A residential school, it was established in 1894 on Brockholes Brow at Farringdon Park, and remained on the site for over 100 years before moving to new premises in Ashton in Ribble. The building is still there and now provides a service for deaf adults.

◄**PRESTON**
Miller Park 1913 65597

Created around 1860 and overlooking the River Ribble, Miller Park is one of several in the town, a welcome contrast to the close-packed housing developments that accompanied Preston's industrial expansion. A lady is pushed along in a wicker bath chair whilst others pause to look at the imposing statue of Edward Stanley, who represented the town in Parliament and became Prime Minister.

▼ **PENWORTHAM,** *The Parish Church 1893* 33088

It is claimed that a church has stood here since 644, although the present building is largely 15th-century. Railings, partly hidden by trees, enclose the tomb of John Horrocks. Born near Bolton in 1768, he established Preston's first cotton mill, known as the Yellow Factory, and founded a textile business that grew to be one of the biggest in the world.

► **HOGHTON**

The Tower 1895 35721

Although the 16th-century buildings have little altered, today's view is quite different, for the garden area is now planted with rose beds set amidst manicured lawns. The de Hoghtons have been here since the Conquest, and the house has had several noteworthy visitors in its time. James I famously knighted 'Sir Loin of Beef' here in 1617 and William Shakespeare performed in the hall.

◄ LONGRIDGE
Berry Lane c1955
L340012

A railway once crossed the road at the bottom of Berry Lane. Its opening in 1848 encouraged the development of the town and an expansion of the nearby quarries, whose fine stone was taken to build Liverpool Docks and the Harris Gallery at Preston. Behind the houses on the left is the 19th-century St Paul's Church.

► CHIPPING
Talbot Street c1955
C598026

In the 18th century, fast flowing streams powered a variety of mills around the village, and many of its cottages date from this period, built to house an expanding work force. But the village had prospered before then, and in one cottage lived John Brabin, a 17th-century cloth merchant and dyer whose wealth founded a school.

WHITEWELL
The Hotel 1921 71247

Now 'The Inn at Whitewell', the place has a reputation for serving
good food and was built towards the end of the 14th century as a
manor house by Walter Urswyck, a Keeper in the Royal Forest. It
also served as the courthouse where the forest law was enforced
and tenants were required to pay their rents, taxes and fines.

▲ WHITEWELL
The Hodder Valley 1921 71244

The point from which this photograph was taken, Seed Hill, was at that time in Yorkshire, but looks over the border, defined here by the Hodder, across a corner of Lancashire. The hills at the back are Mellor Knott and, to the left, Totridge Fell, along which the old border looped, climbing from the river to follow the watershed.

◄ RIBCHESTER
The New Bridge c1955 R29017

Known locally as Dinkley Bridge, this elegant suspension bridge across the River Ribble was opened on 10 October 1951. The crossing, however, is an ancient one, and at one time consisted of two hollowed-out logs pulled across by ropes. The photograph looks to the south bank, where a footpath follows the river downstream through Marles Wood to Salesbury Hall.

▶ **STONYHURST**
The College 1899 43487

Seen from the east across the garden's ornamental pond is the huge façade of Stonyhurst. Begun in 1523 by Hugh Shireburn, it remained the staunchly Catholic family's home until the 18th century, when it passed to the Jesuit order who founded a school here. The priests have since extended the building and added the great church, seen on the left.

◀ STONYHURST
Meteorological Department 1899 43493

In the 19th century the college established an enviable reputation for its scientific studies, producing meteorological and astronomical data to an extremely high standard. So much so, that, in the 1870s, Fathers Perry and Sidgreaves were charged with making official observations of eclipses and other important events including a transit of Venus.

▶ **WHALLEY**
Church Street 1906
54209

Not far from the ruins of Whalley's abbey stands the 13th-century Church of St Mary and All Saints. Amongst the ancient graves surrounding it are three intricately carved Celtic crosses that are some 300 years older than the church. It is said that anyone who can decipher the script on the largest of them will discover the secret of invisibility.

▲ **WHALLEY,** *The Viaduct From The Nab 1901* 47060

This monumental masterpiece of Victorian engineering lies on the railway route between Preston and Hellifield. It required 49 arches to carry the track across the wide Calder Valley, the highest of which are 70 feet above the river. Construction was finally completed in the early 1850s and, at over 600 yards, it is the longest railway viaduct in the country.

WISWELL
The Village 1906 54218

The view looks along the lane towards a 19th-century school
and to the left, down Vicarage Fold, stands the village pub.
The nearby medieval vicarage has a priest hole, often used
during the Catholic persecution that followed the
Reformation, as this, like many other villages in Lancashire
doggedly clung onto the Old Faith.

CLITHEROE
From Castle Street
1921 71132

It is noon, and a convoy of open-topped char à bancs roll into town, no doubt bound for the castle. The hotel on the right has now gone, but the Victoria opposite still serves customers today. Carrying the town's clock is the Carnegie Library, dating from 1905, and behind, in Church Street, is the 19th-century Town Hall.

▶ **CLITHEROE**
Castle Entrance
1921 71136

Above the junction of Castlegate and Parsons Lane is the keep of Clitheroe Castle, which was founded under Roger de Poitou shortly after William seized the throne from Harold. Although most of the castle was destroyed in 1649 after the Civil War, that which remains is classed amongst the county's oldest surviving structures.

◀ **RIBBLE VALLEY**
From Edisford
Bridge 1921 71151

This spot, where the road west from Clitheroe crosses the Ribble, was once known as Eadsford, the bridge from which the photograph was taken being built over an ancient ford. The view looks upstream to Low Moor Mill, which produced cotton cloth until it closed in the 1950s. Its site is now occupied by a housing development.

▲ **WORSTON,** *The Village 1921* 71161

The building on the left was a non-conformist chapel and bears the date 1668, whilst hidden at the end is the Calf's Head. It was reported in a 1906 Rambler Magazine that the Mock Corporation of Worston assembled there under the motto 'Brains Will Tell'. They elected a sham mayor, paying sham debts with sham cheques drawn on a sham bank.

◄ **CHATBURN**
Bridge Road c1955
C462008

Entering the village from Clitheroe, the road dips to cross Heys Brook. Beyond Martin's Bank and the shops is the Black Bull Inn, which carries a date stone of 1855. A little way beyond, set back from the road, is the Brown Cow. Notice the Belisha crossing, they got their name from the minister of transport who introduced them in 1934.

GRINDLETON
The Bridge And The River Ribble 1921 71172

Until 1974, the River Ribble here formed the boundary between Lancashire and Yorkshire, with the bridge carrying the lane between Lancashire's Chatburn and Yorkshire's Grindleton. Notice the arch on the right, built to help ease the passage of water during times of flood. The view upstream beyond the bridge is to Pendle Hill, whose summit is 1,745 feet above sea level.

DOWNHAM
The Village 1921 71182

Picturesque stone cottages line the main street through the village, which climbs from a bridge over Downham Beck to St Leonard's Church. The scene, little changed over the last hundred years, has been a location for 'Whistle Down the Wind' and a BBC drama.

DOWNHAM
Old Inn 1921 71186

The children's hats suggest a hot, sunny summer, as they sit outside the pub opposite St Leonard's Church. It was then known as the George and Dragon, but re-christened the Assheton Arms following the elevation of the squire to Lord Clitheroe. Across the valley rises the massive bulk of Pendle Hill, a prominent feature for miles around.

◄ **SAWLEY**
The Village 1921
71144

Photographed from the Yorkshire bank of the Ribble, the view looks across Sawley to Noddle Hill. The large building at the centre is the Spread Eagle, an inn since the 16th century and probably belonging to the abbey before then. Its riverside location made the pub a popular venue and it was considerably extended during the 1960s to provide a comfortable restaurant.

SAWLEY
Cottages By River Ribble 1921 71147

Not far from Chatburn and Clitheroe, Sawley would have been
a popular day out even before the motor-car was common.
This view, looking downstream towards the abbey, shows
people obviously dressed for a holiday. A girl on the road
wears a hat and shawl, whilst a man in a straw boater walks
with his daughter along the riverbank.

SAWLEY
The Old Gateways 1894 34356

Once known as Salley, the abbey was founded as a Cistercian
community in 1147, the first abbot and monks coming from
Fountains Abbey. These two extravagant arches were later built
using stones from the abbey ruins, but were too narrow to
accommodate modern traffic. They were eventually
demolished following accidents, but one has since been
re-erected in an adjacent field.

THE FYLDE & ITS FRINGES

LYTHAM, *The Sands And Pier 1913* 66441

Hardly a stone's throw from industrial Preston, Lytham's shore and pier were popular destinations for a day-out. The children playing at the water's edge have made a proper occasion of it by bringing a wigwam, and notice the two tots riding on the donkeys; instead of wobbling about on saddles, they sit in the comfortable security of basket-work thrones.

LYTHAM
Lifeboat House 1907
59125

Amongst the facilities provided by the Cliftons was the old lifeboat house, built largely from cobbles and overlooking the promenade wall. Just behind it on the green stands the town's windmill, still a famous landmark. Sited to take full advantage of the winds blowing off the Irish Sea, it was built as a corn mill in about 1805.

LYTHAM, *Central Parade 1894* 33960

The development of many Victorian towns included the provision of a public baths and Lytham is no exception. However, as well as serving a recreational function, they also contributed to the improvement of public health, as most homes still lacked a permanent bathroom and the slipper baths offered the convenience of a hot bath in private.

ST ANNE'S
The Pier 1913 66462

St Anne's was always a 'genteel' place, a mood conveyed here by its Victorian pier that was opened in 1885. Ornate arbours and a Moorish-style pavilion provided seats sheltered from the wind and a floral hall hosted shows and concerts. But crowds must have sometimes been a problem, for signs on the lamp posts direct people to 'keep to the right'.

◄ ST ANNE'S
The Baths 1918 68342

Despite its closeness to the sea, the open-air baths are a popular attraction, but the majority of patrons seem to prefer watching from the poolside or from deckchairs on the balcony above. Modesty still appears to dictate the fashions of bathing attire, with black, one-piece, thigh-length bathing costumes being the order of the day for both sexes.

◀ **ST ANNE'S**
The Sands 1914
67491

From the beach, the pier's extravagant pavilions suggest something mysterious and exotic, a world away from the industry of the nearby towns. On the sands below, Edwardian fashions still predominate; notice the two boys in sailor suits throwing stones at the incoming tide. However, the young mother with the pram looks surprisingly modern, dressed in a cardigan and without a hat.

▲ **ST ANNE'S,** *Model Yacht Pond 1929* 82631

The 'roaring 20s' might almost be over, but the fashions they brought are still evident here. Women, even the matrons, bare ankles and arms, whilst children have discovered a freedom that their doll-like costumed predecessors could only dream of. They are all intent on what is happening on the water as yachts and clockwork boats bob their way around the pool.

◀ **ST ANNE'S**
The Square 1929
82643

The free informality of the boating pool is repeated here, with almost everybody dressed in a more-or-less casual manner. The woman crossing the road might even be setting a trend, her eye-catching coat perhaps anticipating a 1960s musical. Cars and a motor bus line the wide street, where familiar names of today like Boots and Kodak are making an appearance.

FAIRHAVEN
The Lake 1923 74205

Come in number 23, your time is up. However, the shirt-sleeved proprietor seems more intent on his new customer, who is looking over the offered rowing skiff with an apparently knowledgeable eye. Sleek craft such as these, or the sailing dinghy behind, have all but disappeared from today's municipal boating lakes, where pedalos and electric motorboats are now more the fashion.

FAIRHAVEN, *Clifton Drive 1927* 80502

Having held the manor since 1606, the Cliftons were instrumental in its development as a select residential and resort town during the 19th century. Their control over its planning ensured wide streets and an air of comfortable spaciousness. Trams ran along the centre of the main road, and in the background stands the distinctive white Congregationalist church, built in 1912.

FAIRHAVEN
Pollux Gate 1927
80503
Even in the humbler areas of town the same high standards of planning were applied, and wide, uncluttered streets and pavements are a refreshing contrast to the standards favoured by today's developers. The building on the corner houses two large shops, a 'high class' grocer's and, next door, a confectioner's. Opposite is the post office, with a pillar box outside.

BLACKPOOL, *North Pier 1890* 22877

Doubling as a landing stage for steamers, North Pier was the first of Blackpool's three to be built and opened in 1863. Advertised as 'Europe's finest marine parade', it was an instant success, attracting thousands of people each year. Behind the sea-front boarding houses and overlooking Talbot Square is Sacred Heart Church, which was designed by Pugin in 1857.

▶ **BLACKPOOL**
From the South Pier 1890 22868

If you think something is missing amongst the buildings overlooking North Pier you are right, for Blackpool Tower was not begun until 1891. Yet the resort's popularity was already well established and bathing machines and horse-drawn traps line the sands. A wheeled jetty facilitates embarkation for a leisurely sail, whilst the more energetic take their exercise in a rowing boat.

◀**BLACKPOOL**
From The South Pier 1890 22872

Until Blackpool's third pier was built at South Shore in 1893, the one here was known as South Pier. The sea wall had not been built either, and the promenade is bordered by cobbles sloping to the beach, with wooden piles providing some protection against the breaking waves. However, they seem here more profitably employed for drying washing.

▲ **BLACKPOOL,** *Palatine Hotel 1890* 22891

Again, the Tower is conspicuous by its absence in this view of the Palatine Hotel. Built close to both the railway station and beach, it quickly became a successful family hotel. Then, as now, sales and auctions were a popular attraction for holidaymakers, and in the Royal Hotel, a little further along the promenade, was the famous Craven's Sale Room.

◀ **BLACKPOOL**
Winter Gardens 1894
33954

In June 1878, the Lord Mayor of London, Sir Thomas Owen, travelled to Blackpool to open the Winter Gardens. Built to a design by a Manchester architect, it featured a huge dome, 120 feet above an Indian-style lounge. The Floral Hall, a pavilion seating 3,000 people, and the Empress Ballroom were added soon after and it became a major attraction.

BLACKPOOL

From The Central Pier 1896 38845

One of Blackpool's former attractions was a gigantic Ferris wheel, seen here behind the sea-front baths. Constructed in 1896 beside the Winter Gardens, the axle alone accounted for 30 of its 1,000 tons. Before the structure was dismantled in 1928, 30 cars, each accommodating 30 people, rose 220 feet into the air to give a spectacular view across the town.

▼ **BLACKPOOL,** *The Tower 1894* 34798A
The world-famous Tower is nearing completion, but work still continues on the
central staircase. It was inspired by Gustave Eiffel's great tower in Paris, which
had opened five years earlier, but at 518 feet, Blackpool is only a little over half
its height. However, Blackpool's tower boasted a ballroom, permanent circus and
aquarium incorporated within the building at its base.

▶ BLACKPOOL
Sea Front 1901 47037

Before the promenade defences were completed in 1905, Blackpool's sea-front hotels were literally that, with only a narrow road separating them from the waves that crashed onto the beach. Then, as today, horse-drawn carriage rides were popular, as were the electric trams, which were the first operating anywhere in the country and came into service along the promenade in 1885.

▼ BLACKPOOL
Central Pier 1906 53855

Work began on Blackpool's second pier in 1867 and took less than a year to complete. Promoted as the 'pier for the masses', it was hugely popular and offered a variety of entertainments. Here, numerous sign boards displayed around the entrance publicise forthcoming events, whilst some of the hoardings advertise popular brands still around today, Boots the Chemist and Oxo.

▶ CLEVELEYS
The Arena c1955
C440002

The Arena, built below the sea-front promenade, was billed as the 'premier open-air theatre of the north'. During the 1930s it staged three performances every day throughout the season and was a popular attraction for visitors. Here a party of girls, perhaps on a school trip, sit on the wall waiting for the show to begin.

◀**CLEVELEYS**
Princess Walk
c1955 C440004

A quieter resort than neighbouring Blackpool, Cleveleys attracted holidaymakers who were more inclined to stroll along the promenade or sit reading in the sheltered sea-front gardens. Perhaps this lad wishes he were at the fun fair instead, but is apparently making the best of it with a game of marbles whilst his guardian looks on.

▶ **ROSSALL**
Ockwells Caravan Camp c1955 R409009

The Fylde area has long-been popular with holiday-makers, for it is well-sited for day-trips to the Lake District as well as the sea-side resorts of the Blackpool coast. As caravanning grew in popularity during the 1950s, many small sites began to compete with the already established holiday camps, providing facilities, shops and often entertainment in a purpose built club-house.

◀ **FLEETWOOD**
The Esplanade 1892
30423

Although pictured only a century ago, the styles of ladies and children's dress and the high-wheeled pram firmly place the scene in an historical era. The Chinese-style tea-room above the promenade has changed too, being replaced in 1902 by the Mount Pavilion, to which a clock was subsequently added commemorating those killed during the First World War.

▶ **FLEETWOOD**
The Beach 1892
30421.

Then, as now, the beach was popular with children, who here play at the water's edge whilst older boys admire the moored fishing boat. Fleetwood was a busy cargo port too, and the small building above the beach was for the customs officials, who kept tally on the boats moving in and out of the docks.

◀ **FLEETWOOD**
The Harbour 1894
33968

Linked by rail to Euston, Fleetwood developed as a major port, handling passengers and cargo bound for Ireland, the Isle of Man and Glasgow. Berthed at the landing stage is a paddle steamer and around it are clustered some of the small boats that made up the town's famous fishing fleet, which at one time employed over 4,000 men and boys.

▲ **FLEETWOOD,** *The Beach 1902* 49052

To the left, overlooking the beach, stands the lifeboat station and, on the right, one of the town's two lighthouses. It was built in 1840, its lantern originally lit by gas until converted to electrical operation. The second light stands a little way behind, in the town, a much taller tower modelled on the Pharos light of ancient Alexandria.

◀ **KNOTT END-ON-SEA**
The Ferry c1965 K128057

The first Knott End ferry began as a family business shortly after work on Fleetwood started, but in 1894, was taken over by the municipal council. During the resort's heyday it was a popular excursion for visitors and, at one time, the boat carried almost 1½ million passengers a year. Behind is Fleetwood's North Euston Hotel, which opened in 1841.

GARSTANG, *High Street c1950* G238008X

The centre of Garstang has been spared the worst ravages of modern development and, although generally now more busy than depicted here, remains largely unchanged. On the right, surmounted by a balustrade and square clock tower is the town hall and market. Built in 1755, it replaced two previous halls on the same site, both of which had succumbed to fire.

GARSTANG
Bridge Street c1955
G238020

Old rough-stone cottages line the street which leads up to the market place. Just visible is Garstang's market cross, a Tuscan column topped by a stone orb that was erected in 1754. Overlooking it is the Royal Oak Hotel, one of several inns that did well on market days and served coach passengers travelling between Preston and Lancaster.

CHURCHTOWN, *The Village c1955* C603002

The village derives its name from the fact that it was the location of Garstang's parish church, St Helen's, which lies beyond the cottages at the far end of the street. The village cross dates from the 18th century and, at the top of the column on its south-facing aspect, its a sundial, from which the village took its time.

AROUND LANCASTER & THE LUNE VALLEY

LANCASTER, *Town Hall 1903* 50057

Since 1923, this magnificent building has housed the city's fascinating museum, but it opened in 1783 as the corn exchange. The array above the annexe beside the old Town Hall belongs to the telephone exchange, which moved there in 1888. Begun in 1885 with just three lines, the service expanded rapidly, and by 1893, 184 subscribers were generating almost 3,900 calls every week.

▲ **LANCASTER,** *The Town Hall 1912*
64215

At the centre of Dalton Square stands a bronze statue of Queen Victoria guarded by four lions, given to the city by Lord Ashton. He also donated the new Town Hall, which stands at the back. It was opened in 1909 and above its grand portico is a relief that depicts Victoria's successor to the throne, Edward VII.

◄ **LANCASTER,** *Castle Warden 1927*
80507

The warden points to one of the city's landmarks, possibly the Ashton Memorial on the opposite hillside. Almost since its foundation by Roger de Poitou in 1070, the castle has been the seat of justice and punishment; the assizes were held there from 1166 to 1972 and, but for a brief period, has also served as the county jail.

LANCASTER
From Castle Hill
c1950 L10007

Lancaster was an important place throughout the medieval period, but although the pattern of many of its old streets remain, few of today's buildings pre-date the Georgian period. Civil wars, rebellion and border raids all brought destruction before the stability of the mid-18th century, and prosperity from trade with the Indies encouraged investment in grand houses and civic buildings.

LANCASTER, *Penny Street c1950* L10044

Before chain stores dominated Britain's high streets, shoppers could choose from a variety of family traders, as this 1950s street scene illustrates. The sign above Dent's shop, advertising bed and breakfast for cyclists highlights another difference in lifestyles. Few people then had a car, but cycling tours and holidays were a popular way of exploring the countryside.

LANCASTER
Royal Lunatic Asylum
c1878 10699

Later known as the Lancaster Moor Hospital, it opened on 28 July 1816. At first there were only 60 'inmates', but by 1836 the asylum had been extended and could accommodate 406 patients. A report in 1841 identified the causes of insanity for those admitted, which included such things as: 'intoxication', 'epilepsy', 'disappointment in affection, trade or property' and 'hot climate'.

GLASSON, *The Docks c1955* G260012

By the1750s, Lancaster had become the fourth busiest port in the country, but the increasing tonnage of ships and the shallowness of the Lune threatened its downfall. The problem was solved in 1787 by the construction of a three-acre dock here. Warehouses, offices and a customs house sprang up around the quayside, with cottages nearby for the stevedores who handled the cargoes.

▲ GLASSON
The Docks c1955 G260003

A further boost to the port's success came with the construction of a spur to the Lancaster Canal in 1826, and a huge basin was built to accommodate the barges that transported the cargoes inland. Shortly after, a shipyard also opened, and although some new boats were commissioned, it profited more from repairs and refitting work.

▶ BOLTON-LE-SANDS
The Canal 1898 41057

The canal opened in 1817, and ran from Kendal to Lancaster, later continuing south to connect with the Leeds and Liverpool Canal via a tramway at Preston. It was a huge success and even carried passengers on packet boats. The development of the railways heralded its decline, but it was not until 1947 that cargo traffic finally ended.

BOLTON-LE-SANDS, *The Village c1960* B137022

At one time, Co-op shops stood in most towns and even some villages, this one belonging to the Society at nearby Carnforth. Ladies' hairdressers (the shop next door with curtained windows), however, were a less common sight on shopping streets. The imposing building with the portico entrance is the Blue Anchor and, behind, rises the tower of Holy Trinity.

HEST BANK, *The Centre c1960* H453016

Shops and a post office overlook the junction in the centre of the village by the railway station. Just along Station Road, on the left by the chemist is the Marine Café. Well placed to attract passing motorists, it also served the visitors who came to enjoy a day on the shore, where a fine sandy beach borders the sea.

◀ HEST BANK
The Canal c1955
H453003

The Lancaster Canal follows a sinuous course between Tewitfield locks and a splendid aqueduct carrying it across the River Lune, just outside Lancaster. Eventually completed around 1819, it ran for 75 miles between Kendal and Preston. As well as carrying freight, there was a passenger service that completed the journey in less than 14 hours, with refreshments served on board.

◀ MORECAMBE
The Pier 1888 21080

It was only after the railway arrived in 1848 that Morecambe evolved as a resort, developing its own attractions to compete with neighbouring Blackpool. Here, carriages wait to take passengers along the seafront or to the nearby small, inland villages of Bare and Torrisholme. Notice too the young man, sitting on an odd self-propelled machine in front of the carriage.

MORECAMBE
The Sands 1899 42870

There is an element of restraint amongst these holiday-makers, their clothes hardly suited for the occasion as they explore the sands below the stone jetty. A few children are paddling in the water, but further along, adults swim in the sea, having changed in bathing machines that have been brought down by horses to the water's edge.

◀ **MORECAMBE**
*West End Promenade
1899* 42864

Looking north towards the pier, the photograph shows the promenade before the Winter Gardens were built. The tide is well in and horses have been taken down to soak their legs in the salt-water. The hard-working animals seem to enjoy it as much as we do, for it is a break from their labour and helps ease aches and strains.

◄ MORECAMBE
*The Promenade
1899* 42855

The promenade is quite busy, visitors preferring to walk along the seafront rather than settle down on the sand. An open-topped horse-drawn tram travels along the promenade, whilst the kerb is lined with waiting excursion carriages. Several jetties stretch across the sands to the sea, providing moorings and access for pleasure boats and fishing smacks.

▲ **MORECAMBE,** *West End Promenade 1903* 50063

A later view, shows the Winter Gardens now completing the arc of guest houses and other buildings that overlook the wide promenade. People are taking a morning walk along the seafront and, although the day is obviously warm and bright, the fashions of the time keep everybody well-covered up, with many ladies carrying parasols as shade from the sun.

◄ MORECAMBE
*Central Promenade
c1950* M94023

Barely 50 years later, the scene is altogether different. Car ownership is no longer confined to the rich, and the mass-produced, 'sit-up-and-beg' vehicles were now a common sight on the road. A cheaper alternative that gave the same independence, if not the comfort, was a motorbike, and, if you had a family, just tag on a sidecar.

▶ **HEYSHAM,** *Cosy Corner c1900*
H81301

Lying close to the larger holiday centre of Morecambe, Heysham has been popular with visitors since the Victorian period, many coming to sample the famous locally brewed nettle beer. In consequence, several of the ancient cottages opened their doors as tea-rooms and cafes, offering lunches and high teas of home-made cakes and biscuits.

▼ **HEYSHAM,** *The Foreshore c1947* H81003

With the return of peace, people could again enjoy seaside holidays and once more flocked to the Lancashire resorts. Cars, motorbikes and sidecars are parked on the beach, whilst their owners clamber over the rocks or paddle in the sea. However, those by the slipway appear rather formally dressed and have perhaps made a brief stop during a coach tour.

▶ **HEYSHAM**
Main Street 1947
H81005

Heysham old village is an attractive place, with an assortment of stone cottages lining the streets. Visitors wander past the shops and the ancient Royal Hotel, whilst their excursion bus waits at the far end. Outside the barn a photographer waits for customers, as few people then had a camera of their own with which to record the family's day out.

◄ **HEYSHAM**
Half Moon Bay
c1965 H81027

Before the advent of cheap, foreign package holidays, Lancashire resorts and beaches continued to draw summer crowds, with donkeys and deckchairs here completing a traditional British scene. Many of the people enjoying the sands below Heysham Head would be staying at the nearby holiday camp, which offered an 'all-in' break, with meals and nightly dancing or variety shows included.

◀HEYSHAM
Stone Coffins 1912
64229

Nobody knows for sure when these graves were painstakingly cut from the sandstone bedrock beside the chapel, but it is likely that they date from the 8th century and were the resting places of monks or perhaps local chieftains. Carved lids once covered the coffin-shaped burials and the sockets at the head of each grave supported stone crosses.

◀ **HEYSHAM**
St Patrick's Chapel Ruins 1888 21071

Victorian ladies sit amongst the enigmatic ruins of this tiny chapel, which perches above low cliffs overlooking the sea near Heysham. Perhaps the earliest Christian church in the North-west, it is supposedly built upon the spot where St Patrick was shipwrecked at the beginning of the 5th century, whilst attempting to reach Scotland from Ireland.

▲ **HALTON,** *The Village c1960* H506052

But for its battlements, the tower would hardly clear the roof of St Wilfrid's Church. One of the county's earliest churches, it was founded in the 7th century and has several Saxon crosses, one carved with both pagan and Christian symbols. It seems the building occupied an even older sacred site, for a Roman altar was unearthed there in 1794.

◀ **CATON**
The Druids Oak c1955 C473013

Beneath the ancient oak are the 'fish stones', steps of a market cross on which monks from nearby Gresgarth displayed their catches for sale. Agriculture dominated the village until the end of the 17th century, when Arkle Beck was harnessed for cotton mills. Low Mill, which only closed in 1970, was claimed to be the oldest in the country.

CATON
Gresgarth Hall
c1955 C473020

Standing in its own grounds, this fine house is thought to have been built as a monks' rest-house at the end of the 12th century for the convenience of the abbot of Furness when visiting his estates in Yorkshire. Although parts of the original building remain, it has been much altered and added to over the years.

BROOKHOUSE, *The Village c1955* B872003

But for the dress of the visitors, this picture might have been taken 60 years earlier. At the top of the street is St Paul's Church, there since 1230, but considerably rebuilt in the middle of the 19th century. By Bull Beck Bridge is the Black Bull Inn, where a cat sits beside a boot-scraper, perhaps waiting for opening time?

▶ **BROOKHOUSE**
Bull Beck c1955
B872058

Perhaps it is Monday, for the washing is out, and from the nappies there seems to be a baby in the family. Without automatic machines, it was an all-day job; washing, rinsing, blueing and mangling, and then pegging out before the rain came. After that, the ironing still had to be done, usually the same evening whilst listening to the radio.

◀ **HORNBY**
The Castle c1910
H454020

Originating from a 13th-century pele tower, the castle was largely rebuilt as a stately home during the 18th century. One owner, Sir Edward Stanley, fought at Flodden in 1513 and was subsequently created Lord Mounteagle for his valiant service. It is said that he built the tower of nearby St Margaret's Church as a thanksgiving for his safe return.

► **CARNFORTH**
Market Street
1898 41032

Already busy with turnpike traffic, the railway's arrival encouraged more hotels, such as the Royal Station Hotel at the bottom of the street. On the corner is Woolstencroft's chemist, notice the apothecary jars in the window and a mortar and pestle above its entrance. Look too at a sign etched on the glass of the door, 'TEETH CAREFULLY EXTRACTED'.

◄ **WARTON**
The Crag 1898 41041

Along Borwick Lane, past the wooden-shuttered windows of a Methodist chapel, is the small village of Warton. Behind rises a jagged escarpment, Warton Crag, a natural stronghold that has attracted man since the earliest times. Its caves have revealed objects from the late Stone Age to the Roman period and on its summit is a fort built by the Brigantes.

▲ **WARTON,** *The Village 1897* 40501

Dominating the village is the 15th-century church of St Oswald's, its tower gifted by Robert Washington. The family arrived from Durham in the 13th century and were ancestors of George Washington, America's first president. The Washington coat-of-arms, three mullets and two bars, can be found in the church and the stars and stripes are flown from the tower on Independence Day.

◀ **YEALAND CONYERS**
The Village 1898 41052

The origins of this rambling building, which overlooks the main street, lie in a 15th-century farmhouse, and until the New Inn was built in the 1640s, it also served the village as its ale-house. The original cottage was 'gentrified' during the early 19th century and later, the local doctor added extensions, which he used as his waiting room and surgery.

SILVERDALE
Emesgate Lane c1960 S609034

A pleasant setting against a backdrop of wooded hills and a
gentle coastline with wonderful views to the southern Lakes
helped establish Silverdale as a quietly fashionable medicinal
sea-bathing resort during the latter part of the 19th century.
Spacious period houses line its streets and lanes, built by the
affluent who came then, as now, to retire here.

LANCASHIRE OVER THE SANDS

GRANGE-OVER-SANDS, *Main Street 1891* 28638

Until the railway arrived, only 35 years before this photograph was taken, Grange-over-Sands was little more than a fishing village, looking out across the Kent estuary to the rest of Lancashire. No longer reliant on a hazardous route across the sands, the town quickly grew, catering for the well-to-do, who came here to live or take their holidays.

109

◄ CARTMEL
Gatehouse And Market Cross 1921
70707

Overlooking the square is an arched gatehouse, built in the 14th century as a defence against Scottish raiders. It also served as the manorial courthouse but, during the 17th and 18th centuries housed a grammar school and later served as a general store. The gatehouse and the nearby church are all that remain of Cartmel's 12th-century Augustinian priory.

◀ **GRANGE-OVER-SANDS**
Main Street 1912
64360

Twenty years later, the scene is much the same, although the street has now been sealed with a tarmacadam surface. On the right, occupying part of the Victoria Hall are the premises of the London City and Midland Bank. The hall itself was opened in 1901, as part of the town's commemoration of Queen Victoria's diamond jubilee.

▲ **CARTMEL,** *Priory Church And Beck 1894* 34095

This fine clapper bridge has gone, but not the Methodist church to the right, which was completed two decades before the photograph was taken. Behind is the former priory church, its cross-set belfry rising above a low square tower. It was spared the destruction that befell the rest of the monastery at the Dissolution, because the town claimed it as their parish church.

◀ **ULVERSTON**
Mearness Sands 1921
70695

Taken from above the mouth of the River Leven, this view overlooks Greenodd Sands towards Ulverston. In the distance, a 100ft tower, a replica of the famous Eddystone Lighthouse, surmounts Hoad Hill. It is a monument to John Barrow, one-time Secretary of the Admiralty and a great traveller, who founded the Royal Geographical Society in 1830.

ULVERSTON
The Square 1895
35896

A market town since the 13th century, Ulverston became a busy port during the 18th and 19th centuries, exporting slate via the country's shortest canal. A wonderful variety of shops surround the Square as well as several pubs. One of them, the Sun, still carries a sign authorising extended opening hours to serve people attending the cattle and general weekly markets.

CONISTON, *Lake From Beacon's Crag 1929* 82789

This is the land of Swallows and Amazons, for near the foot of Coniston Water lies High Nibthwaite, where the author, Arthur Ransome spent his childhood holidays and developed a passion for the area that was to last throughout his life. Beyond the promontories of Park Nab and High Peel Near is Peel Island, renamed 'Wild Cat Island' in his famous tales.

▶ **CONISTON**
View On The Tilberthwaite Road 1912 64273

For a short time in the middle of the 19th century, copper was mined in Dry Cove above Tilberthwaite. More important were the many stone quarries, from which was cut a fine green slate that has been used around the world. There is no hint of that industry, though, in this timeless picture, where children play by the waterside.

◀ **HAWKSHEAD** *And Wetherlam 1929* 82362

Beyond the village rises Wetherlam, the most northerly of the Coniston Fells, and over to the left, hidden by cloud, Lancashire's highest peak, the Old Man. Prominent above Hawkshead is St Michael and All Angels' Church, of which William Wordsworth wrote '..I saw a snow white church upon her hill, sit like a throned lady...'

HAWKSHEAD
The Old Courthouse 1896 38835

Built in the 15th century as a gatehouse to Hawkshead Hall,
which was then a grange belonging to Furness Abbey, the Old
Courthouse has served many other purposes including
stabling and a church. A niche above the gateway once held a
figure of the Virgin Mary and below, much worn by the
passage of time, is carved a lion's head.

INDEX

Frith Book Co Titles

www.francisfrith.co.uk

The Frith Book Company publishes over 100 new titles each year. A selection of those currently available are listed below. For latest catalogue please contact Frith Book Co.
Town Books 96 pages, approximately 100 photos. **County and Themed Books** 128 pages, approximately 150 photos (unless specified). All titles hardback with laminated case and jacket, except those indicated pb (paperback)

Amersham, Chesham & Rickmansworth (pb)	1-85937-340-2	£9.99	Devon (pb)	1-85937-297-x	£9.99
Andover (pb)	1-85937-292-9	£9.99	Devon Churches (pb)	1-85937-250-3	£9.99
Aylesbury (pb)	1-85937-227-9	£9.99	Dorchester (pb)	1-85937-307-0	£9.99
Barnstaple (pb)	1-85937-300-3	£9.99	Dorset (pb)	1-85937-269-4	£9.99
Basildon Living Memories (pb)	1-85937-515-4	£9.99	Dorset Coast (pb)	1-85937-299-6	£9.99
Bath (pb)	1-85937-419-0	£9.99	Dorset Living Memories (pb)	1-85937-584-7	£9.99
Bedford (pb)	1-85937-205-8	£9.99	Down the Severn (pb)	1-85937-560-x	£9.99
Bedfordshire Living Memories	1-85937-513-8	£14.99	Down The Thames (pb)	1-85937-278-3	£9.99
Belfast (pb)	1-85937-303-8	£9.99	Down the Trent	1-85937-311-9	£14.99
Berkshire (pb)	1-85937-191-4	£9.99	East Anglia (pb)	1-85937-265-1	£9.99
Berkshire Churches	1-85937-170-1	£17.99	East Grinstead (pb)	1-85937-138-8	£9.99
Berkshire Living Memories	1-85937-332-1	£14.99	East London	1-85937-080-2	£14.99
Black Country	1-85937-497-2	£12.99	East Sussex (pb)	1-85937-606-1	£9.99
Blackpool (pb)	1-85937-393-3	£9.99	Eastbourne (pb)	1-85937-399-2	£9.99
Bognor Regis (pb)	1-85937-431-x	£9.99	Edinburgh (pb)	1-85937-193-0	£8.99
Bournemouth (pb)	1-85937-545-6	£9.99	England In The 1880s	1-85937-331-3	£17.99
Bradford (pb)	1-85937-204-x	£9.99	Essex - Second Selection	1-85937-456-5	£14.99
Bridgend (pb)	1-85937-386-0	£7.99	Essex (pb)	1-85937-270-8	£9.99
Bridgwater (pb)	1-85937-305-4	£9.99	Essex Coast	1-85937-342-9	£14.99
Bridport (pb)	1-85937-327-5	£9.99	Essex Living Memories	1-85937-490-5	£14.99
Brighton (pb)	1-85937-192-2	£8.99	Exeter	1-85937-539-1	£9.99
Bristol (pb)	1-85937-264-3	£9.99	Exmoor (pb)	1-85937-608-8	£9.99
British Life A Century Ago (pb)	1-85937-213-9	£9.99	Falmouth (pb)	1-85937-594-4	£9.99
Buckinghamshire (pb)	1-85937-200-7	£9.99	Folkestone (pb)	1-85937-124-8	£9.99
Camberley (pb)	1-85937-222-8	£9.99	Frome (pb)	1-85937-317-8	£9.99
Cambridge (pb)	1-85937-422-0	£9.99	Glamorgan	1-85937-488-3	£14.99
Cambridgeshire (pb)	1-85937-420-4	£9.99	Glasgow (pb)	1-85937-190-6	£9.99
Cambridgeshire Villages	1-85937-523-5	£14.99	Glastonbury (pb)	1-85937-338-0	£7.99
Canals And Waterways (pb)	1-85937-291-0	£9.99	Gloucester (pb)	1-85937-232-5	£9.99
Canterbury Cathedral (pb)	1-85937-179-5	£9.99	Gloucestershire (pb)	1-85937-561-8	£9.99
Cardiff (pb)	1-85937-093-4	£9.99	Great Yarmouth (pb)	1-85937-426-3	£9.99
Carmarthenshire (pb)	1-85937-604-5	£9.99	Greater Manchester (pb)	1-85937-266-x	£9.99
Chelmsford (pb)	1-85937-310-0	£9.99	Guildford (pb)	1-85937-410-7	£9.99
Cheltenham (pb)	1-85937-095-0	£9.99	Hampshire (pb)	1-85937-279-1	£9.99
Cheshire (pb)	1-85937-271-6	£9.99	Harrogate (pb)	1-85937-423-9	£9.99
Chester (pb)	1-85937-382 8	£9.99	Hastings and Bexhill (pb)	1-85937-131-0	£9.99
Chesterfield (pb)	1-85937-378-x	£9.99	Heart of Lancashire (pb)	1-85937-197-3	£9.99
Chichester (pb)	1-85937-228-7	£9.99	Helston (pb)	1-85937-214-7	£9.99
Churches of East Cornwall (pb)	1-85937-249-x	£9.99	Hereford (pb)	1-85937-175-2	£9.99
Churches of Hampshire (pb)	1-85937-207-4	£9.99	Herefordshire (pb)	1-85937-567-7	£9.99
Cinque Ports & Two Ancient Towns	1-85937-492-1	£14.99	Herefordshire Living Memories	1-85937-514-6	£14.99
Colchester (pb)	1-85937-188-4	£8.99	Hertfordshire (pb)	1-85937-247-3	£9.99
Cornwall (pb)	1-85937-229-5	£9.99	Horsham (pb)	1-85937-432-8	£9.99
Cornwall Living Memories	1-85937-248-1	£14.99	Humberside (pb)	1-85937-605-3	£9.99
Cotswolds (pb)	1-85937-230-9	£9.99	Hythe, Romney Marsh, Ashford (pb)	1-85937-256-2	£9.99
Cotswolds Living Memories	1-85937-255-4	£14.99	Ipswich (pb)	1-85937-424-7	£9.99
County Durham (pb)	1-85937-398-4	£9.99	Isle of Man (pb)	1-85937-268-6	£9.99
Croydon Living Memories (pb)	1-85937-162-0	£9.99	Isle of Wight (pb)	1-85937-429-8	£9.99
Cumbria (pb)	1-85937-621-5	£9.99	Isle of Wight Living Memories	1-85937-304-6	£14.99
Derby (pb)	1-85937-367-4	£9.99	Kent (pb)	1-85937-189-2	£9.99
Derbyshire (pb)	1-85937-196-5	£9.99	Kent Living Memories(pb)	1-85937-401-8	£9.99
Derbyshire Living Memories	1-85937-330-5	£14.99	Kings Lynn (pb)	1-85937-334-8	£9.99

Available from your local bookshop or from the publisher

Frith Book Co Titles (continued)

Title	ISBN	Price	Title	ISBN	Price
Lake District (pb)	1-85937-275-9	£9.99	Sherborne (pb)	1-85937-301-1	£9.99
Lancashire Living Memories	1-85937-335-6	£14.99	Shrewsbury (pb)	1-85937-325-9	£9.99
Lancaster, Morecambe, Heysham (pb)	1-85937-233-3	£9.99	Shropshire (pb)	1-85937-326-7	£9.99
Leeds (pb)	1-85937-202-3	£9.99	Shropshire Living Memories	1-85937-643-6	£14.99
Leicester (pb)	1-85937-381-x	£9.99	Somerset	1-85937-153-1	£14.99
Leicestershire & Rutland Living Memories	1-85937-500-6	£12.99	South Devon Coast	1-85937-107-8	£14.99
Leicestershire (pb)	1-85937-185-x	£9.99	South Devon Living Memories (pb)	1-85937-609-6	£9.99
Lighthouses	1-85937-257-0	£9.99	South East London (pb)	1-85937-263-5	£9.99
Lincoln (pb)	1-85937-380-1	£9.99	South Somerset	1-85937-318-6	£14.99
Lincolnshire (pb)	1-85937-433-6	£9.99	South Wales	1-85937-519-7	£14.99
Liverpool and Merseyside (pb)	1-85937-234-1	£9.99	Southampton (pb)	1-85937-427-1	£9.99
London (pb)	1-85937-183-3	£9.99	Southend (pb)	1-85937-313-5	£9.99
London Living Memories	1-85937-454-9	£14.99	Southport (pb)	1-85937-425-5	£9.99
Ludlow (pb)	1-85937-176-0	£9.99	St Albans (pb)	1-85937-341-0	£9.99
Luton (pb)	1-85937-235-x	£9.99	St Ives (pb)	1-85937-415-8	£9.99
Maidenhead (pb)	1-85937-339-9	£9.99	Stafford Living Memories (pb)	1-85937-503-0	£9.99
Maidstone (pb)	1-85937-391-7	£9.99	Staffordshire (pb)	1-85937-308-9	£9.99
Manchester (pb)	1-85937-198-1	£9.99	Stourbridge (pb)	1-85937-530-8	£9.99
Marlborough (pb)	1-85937-336-4	£9.99	Stratford upon Avon (pb)	1-85937-388-7	£9.99
Middlesex	1-85937-158-2	£14.99	Suffolk (pb)	1-85937-221-x	£9.99
Monmouthshire	1-85937-532-4	£14.99	Suffolk Coast (pb)	1-85937-610-x	£9.99
New Forest (pb)	1-85937-390-9	£9.99	Surrey (pb)	1-85937-240-6	£9.99
Newark (pb)	1-85937-366-6	£9.99	Surrey Living Memories	1-85937-328-3	£14.99
Newport, Wales (pb)	1-85937-258-9	£9.99	Sussex (pb)	1-85937-184-1	£9.99
Newquay (pb)	1-85937-421-2	£9.99	Sutton (pb)	1-85937-337-2	£9.99
Norfolk (pb)	1-85937-195-7	£9.99	Swansea (pb)	1-85937-167-1	£9.99
Norfolk Broads	1-85937-486-7	£14.99	Taunton (pb)	1-85937-314-3	£9.99
Norfolk Living Memories (pb)	1-85937-402-6	£9.99	Tees Valley & Cleveland (pb)	1-85937-623-1	£9.99
North Buckinghamshire	1-85937-626-6	£14.99	Teignmouth (pb)	1-85937-370-4	£7.99
North Devon Living Memories	1-85937-261-9	£14.99	Thanet (pb)	1-85937-116-7	£9.99
North Hertfordshire	1-85937-547-2	£14.99	Tiverton (pb)	1-85937-178-7	£9.99
North London (pb)	1-85937-403-4	£9.99	Torbay (pb)	1-85937-597-9	£9.99
North Somerset	1-85937-302-x	£14.99	Truro (pb)	1-85937-598-7	£9.99
North Wales (pb)	1-85937-298-8	£9.99	Victorian & Edwardian Dorset	1-85937-254-6	£14.99
North Yorkshire (pb)	1-85937-236-8	£9.99	Victorian & Edwardian Kent (pb)	1-85937-624-X	£9.99
Northamptonshire Living Memories	1-85937-529-4	£14.99	Victorian & Edwardian Maritime Album (pb)	1-85937-622-3	£9.99
Northamptonshire	1-85937-150-7	£14.99	Victorian and Edwardian Sussex (pb)	1-85937-625-8	£9.99
Northumberland Tyne & Wear (pb)	1-85937-281-3	£9.99	Villages of Devon (pb)	1-85937-293-7	£9.99
Northumberland	1-85937-522-7	£14.99	Villages of Kent (pb)	1-85937-294-5	£9.99
Norwich (pb)	1-85937-194-9	£8.99	Villages of Sussex (pb)	1-85937-295-3	£9.99
Nottingham (pb)	1-85937-324-0	£9.99	Warrington (pb)	1-85937-507-3	£9.99
Nottinghamshire (pb)	1-85937-187-6	£9.99	Warwick (pb)	1-85937-518-9	£9.99
Oxford (pb)	1-85937-411-5	£9.99	Warwickshire (pb)	1-85937-203-1	£9.99
Oxfordshire (pb)	1-85937-430-1	£9.99	Welsh Castles (pb)	1-85937-322-4	£9.99
Oxfordshire Living Memories	1-85937-525-1	£14.99	West Midlands (pb)	1-85937-289-9	£9.99
Paignton (pb)	1-85937-374-7	£7.99	West Sussex (pb)	1-85937-607-x	£9.99
Peak District (pb)	1-85937-280-5	£9.99	West Yorkshire (pb)	1-85937-201-5	£9.99
Pembrokeshire	1-85937-262-7	£14.99	Weston Super Mare (pb)	1-85937-306-2	£9.99
Penzance (pb)	1-85937-595-2	£9.99	Weymouth (pb)	1-85937-209-0	£9.99
Peterborough (pb)	1-85937-219-8	£9.99	Wiltshire (pb)	1-85937-277-5	£9.99
Picturesque Harbours	1-85937-208-2	£14.99	Wiltshire Churches (pb)	1-85937-171-x	£9.99
Piers	1-85937-237-6	£17.99	Wiltshire Living Memories (pb)	1-85937-396-8	£9.99
Plymouth (pb)	1-85937-389-5	£9.99	Winchester (pb)	1-85937-428-x	£9.99
Poole & Sandbanks (pb)	1-85937-251-1	£9.99	Windsor (pb)	1-85937-333-x	£9.99
Preston (pb)	1-85937-212-0	£9.99	Wokingham & Bracknell (pb)	1-85937-329-1	£9.99
Reading (pb)	1-85937-238-4	£9.99	Woodbridge (pb)	1-85937-498-0	£9.99
Redhill to Reigate (pb)	1-85937-596-0	£9.99	Worcester (pb)	1-85937-165-5	£9.99
Ringwood (pb)	1-85937-384-4	£7.99	Worcestershire Living Memories	1-85937-489-1	£14.99
Romford (pb)	1-85937-319-4	£9.99	Worcestershire	1-85937-152-3	£14.99
Royal Tunbridge Wells (pb)	1-85937-504-9	£9.99	York (pb)	1-85937-199-x	£9.99
Salisbury (pb)	1-85937-239-2	£9.99	Yorkshire (pb)	1-85937-186-8	£9.99
Scarborough (pb)	1-85937-379-8	£9.99	Yorkshire Coastal Memories	1-85937-506-5	£14.99
Sevenoaks and Tonbridge (pb)	1-85937-392-5	£9.99	Yorkshire Dales	1-85937-502-2	£14.99
Sheffield & South Yorks (pb)	1-85937-267-8	£9.99	Yorkshire Living Memories (pb)	1-85937-397-6	£9.99

See Frith books on the internet at www.francisfrith.co.uk

FRITH PRODUCTS & SERVICES

Francis Frith would doubtless be pleased to know that the pioneering publishing venture he started in 1860 still continues today. Over a hundred and forty years later, The Francis Frith Collection continues in the same innovative tradition and is now one of the foremost publishers of vintage photographs in the world. Some of the current activities include:

Interior Decoration

Today Frith's photographs can be seen framed and as giant wall murals in thousands of pubs, restaurants, hotels, banks, retail stores and other public buildings throughout the country. In every case they enhance the unique local atmosphere of the places they depict and provide reminders of gentler days in an increasingly busy and frenetic world.

Product Promotions

Frith products are used by many major companies to promote the sales of their own products or to reinforce their own history and heritage. Frith promotions have been used by Hovis bread, Courage beers, Scots Porage Oats, Colman's mustard, Cadbury's foods, Mellow Birds coffee, Dunhill pipe tobacco, Guinness, and Bulmer's Cider.

Genealogy and Family History

As the interest in family history and roots grows world-wide, more and more people are turning to Frith's photographs of Great Britain for images of the towns, villages and streets where their ancestors lived; and, of course, photographs of the churches and chapels where their ancestors were christened, married and buried are an essential part of every genealogy tree and family album.

Frith Products

All Frith photographs are available Framed or just as Mounted Prints and Posters (size 23 x 16 inches). These may be ordered from the address below. From time to time other products - Address Books, Calendars, Table Mats, etc - are available.

The Internet

Already fifty thousand Frith photographs can be viewed and purchased on the internet through the Frith websites and a myriad of partner sites.

For more detailed information on Frith companies and products, look at these sites:

www.francisfrith.co.uk
www.francisfrith.com
(for North American visitors)

See the complete list of Frith Books at:

www.francisfrith.co.uk

This web site is regularly updated with the latest list of publications from the Frith Book Company. If you wish to buy books relating to another part of the country that your local bookshop does not stock, you may purchase on-line.

For further information, trade, or author enquiries please contact us at the address below:
The Francis Frith Collection, Frith's Barn, Teffont, Salisbury, Wiltshire, England SP3 5QP.
Tel: +44 (0)1722 716 376 Fax: +44 (0)1722 716 881 Email: sales@francisfrith.co.uk

See Frith books on the internet at www.francisfrith.co.uk

HOW TO ORDER YOUR FREE MOUNTED PRINT
and other Frith prints at half price

Mounted Print
Overall size 14 x 11 inches

*Fill in and cut out this voucher and return it
with your remittance for £2.25 (to cover
postage and handling to UK addresses).
For overseas addresses please include £4.00
post and handling.
Choose any photograph included in this book.
Your SEPIA print will be A4 in size. It will be
mounted in a cream mount with a burgundy
rule line (overall size 14 x 11 inches).*

Order additional Mounted Prints
at HALF PRICE (only £7.49 each*)
If you would like to order more Frith prints
from this book, possibly as gifts for friends
and family, you can buy them at half price
(with no additional postage and handling
costs).

Have your Mounted Prints framed
For an extra £14.95 per print* you can have
your mounted print(s) framed in an elegant
polished wood and gilt moulding, overall
size 16 x 13 inches (no additional postage
and handling required).

---

* IMPORTANT!

These special prices are only available if you
order at the same time as you order your free
mounted print. You must use the ORIGINAL
VOUCHER on this page (no copies permitted).
We can only despatch to one address.

 *for FREE* and Reduced Price Frith Prints

*Please do not photocopy this voucher. Only the original is valid,
so please fill it in, cut it out and return it to us with your order.*

Picture ref no	Page number	Qty	Mounted @ £7.49	Framed + £14.95	Total Cost
		1	Free of charge*	£	£
			£7.49	£	£
			£7.49	£	£
			£7.49	£	£
			£7.49	£	£
			£7.49	£	£
Please allow 28 days for delivery			* Post & handling (UK)		£2.25
			Total Order Cost		£

Title of this book . . . .

I enclose a cheque/postal order for £ . . . .
made payable to 'The Francis Frith Collection'

OR please debit my Mastercard / Visa / Switch / Amex card
(credit cards please on all overseas orders), details below

Card Number

Issue No (Switch only)   Valid from (Amex/Switch)

Expires   Signature

Name Mr/Mrs/Ms . . . .

Address . . . .

. . . .

. . . .

. . . . Postcode . . . .

Daytime Tel No . . . .

Email . . . .

Valid to 31/12/05

Send completed Voucher form to:
The Francis Frith Collection, Frith's Barn, Teffont, Salisbury, Wiltshire SP3 5QP

Would you like to find out more about Francis Frith?

We have recently recruited some entertaining speakers who are happy to visit local groups, clubs and societies to give an illustrated talk documenting Frith's travels and photographs. If you are a member of such a group and are interested in hosting a presentation, we would love to hear from you.

Our speakers bring with them a small selection of our local town and county books, together with sample prints. They are happy to take orders. A small proportion of the order value is donated to the group who have hosted the presentation. The talks are therefore an excellent way of fundraising for small groups and societies.

Can you help us with information about any of the Frith photographs in this book?

We are gradually compiling an historical record for each of the photographs in the Frith archive. It is always fascinating to find out the names of the people shown in the pictures, as well as insights into the shops, buildings and other features depicted.

If you recognize anyone in the photographs in this book, or if you have information not already included in the author's caption, do let us know. We would love to hear from you, and will try to publish it in future books or articles.

Our production team

Frith books are produced by a small dedicated team at offices in the converted Grade II listed 18th-century barn at Teffont near Salisbury, illustrated above. Most have worked with the Frith Collection for many years. All have in common one quality: they have a passion for the Frith Collection. The team is constantly expanding, but currently includes:

Jason Buck, John Buck, Douglas Burns, Ruth Butler, Heather Crisp, Isobel Hall, Hazel Heaton, Peter Horne, James Kinnear, Tina Leary, Sue Molloy, Hannah Marsh, Kate Rotondetto, Dean Scource, Eliza Sackett, Terence Sackett, Sandra Sanger, Lewis Taylor, and Shelley Tolcher.

FESTIVALS OF THE WORLD
INDIA

W

FRANKLIN WATTS
LONDON • SYDNEY

This edition first published in 2006 by
Franklin Watts
338 Euston Road
London
NW1 3BH

This edition is published for sale only in the United
Kingdom & Eire.

© Marshall Cavendish International (Asia) Pte Ltd 2006
Originated and designed by Marshall Cavendish
International (Asia) Pte Ltd
A member of Times Publishing Limited
Times Centre, 1 New Industrial Road
Singapore 536196

Written by: Falaq Kagda
Edited by: Katharine Brown-Carpenter
Designed by: Jean Tan
Picture research: Thomas Khoo and Joshua Ang

A CIP catalogue record for this book is available from
the British Library.

ISBN 0 7496 6771 0

Dewey Classification: 394.26954

Printed in Malaysia

CONTENTS

It's Festival Time . . .

Whatever your religion, whoever you are, there are plenty of festivals for you in India. Whether you're Muslim or Sikh or Christian, farmer or merchant, there's a festival specially for you. And with every festival, there's a **mela** that goes with it (that means "fair" in **Hindi**). Come along, take a ride on the Ferris wheel, go on an elephant ride (or do you prefer camels?) and buy some pretty jewellery. Put on your best clothes because it's festival time in India . . .

WHERE'S INDIA?

India takes up most of southern Asia. It is a huge country and more crowded than almost anywhere else in the world. One person in every six people on Earth lives in India. The country has everything from the highest mountain range in the world on its northern border to hot tropical jungles in the south. At the heart of India is the Ganges river, which brings life to the plains around it. The Ganges is sacred to Indians. The capital is New Delhi. India also has other very large and crowded cities, such as Calcutta and Bombay.

Who are the Indians?

There are many different kinds of people in India. Those in the South are smaller and darker than those in the North, and there are many variations in between. Long ago, **Caucasians** moved from Persia into India, where the dark-skinned **Dravidians** were already living. Over the centuries, they have mixed and created people of many different colours and features. Indians speak a variety of languages and have widely different customs. Most Indians are Hindus, but there are also many Muslims, Sikhs, Christians, Buddhists and Jains.

A smiling Indian girl wears a garland of flowers, ready to go to a festival.

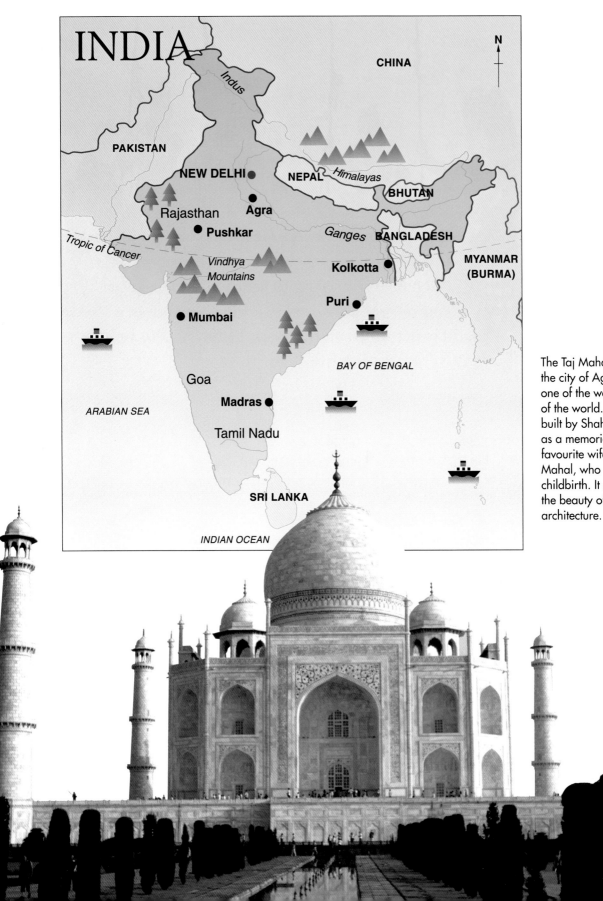

INDIA

N

CHINA

PAKISTAN

Indus

NEW DELHI ●

NEPAL *Himalayas*

BHUTAN

Rajasthan

Agra

● **Pushkar**

Ganges **BANGLADESH**

Tropic of Cancer

MYANMAR (BURMA)

Vindhya Mountains

Kolkotta ●

Puri ●

● **Mumbai**

BAY OF BENGAL

Goa

ARABIAN SEA

Madras ●

Tamil Nadu

SRI LANKA

INDIAN OCEAN

The Taj Mahal, near the city of Agra, is one of the wonders of the world. It was built by Shah Jehan as a memorial to his favourite wife, Mumtaz Mahal, who died in childbirth. It shows the beauty of Islamic architecture.

WHEN'S THE MELA?

Indians use three different calendars. Hindu festivals follow a special **lunar** calendar. This calendar follows the phases of the moon. The dates of these festivals change from year to year on the Gregorian calendar (that's the one you're probably used to). Muslims follow a different lunar calendar. Their festivals move back 11 days every year, so they aren't even in the same season from year to year.

SPRING

Want some colour in your life? Join me for Holi on page 16.

- ✪ **BASANT** – For this celebration of spring, people wear something yellow. Often there are kite-flying competitions.
- ✪ **MAHAVIR JAYANTI** – Celebrates the birthday of Vardhamana Mahavira, who started the Jain religion. Jains come from all over to visit their shrine at Gimar. ✪ **HOLI** ✪ **POORAM**
- ✪ **BAISAKHI** – Sikhs celebrate the New Year at this time. They have a big meal together at the temple, then dance the ***bhangra*** in the streets in the evening (look at page 11 to see the bhangra).

SUMMER

- ✪ **RATHA JATRA** (The Chariot Festival) – Images of Krishna and his family are dragged through the streets of Puri on huge chariots. It takes 4,000 people to pull one of these chariots.
- ✪ **INDEPENDENCE DAY**
- ✪ **RAKSHA BANDHAN**
- ✪ **NAAG PANCHAMI**

Come monkey around with the animals on page 20.

AUTUMN

- ✪ **DUSSEHRA** – The festival of the mother goddess, Durga. Statues of Durga are carried to the Ganges River and thrown in.
- ✪ **DIVALI** ✪ **PUSHKAR MELA**
- ✪ **GANDHI JAYANTI** – Celebrates Gandhi's birthday (2 October).

The Republic Day celebration starts on page 8.

WINTER

- ✪ **GURU NANAK JAYANTI** – Sikhs celebrate the birthday of Guru Nanak, who started Sikhism. ✪ **REPUBLIC DAY** ✪ **PONGAL**
- ✪ **CARNIVAL** – Christians in Goa celebrate Carnival with a traditional red-and-black dance, where they wear all red and black.

MUSLIM HOLIDAYS

- ✪ **MUHARRAM** – The anniversary of the day the Prophet Muhammad left for Medina, which marks the beginning of the Islamic religion. There are processions in honour of Husain, the Prophet's grandson, who was killed on this day.
- ✪ **ID-UL-FITRI** – Marks the end of the fasting month of Ramadhan. People wear new clothes and have big feasts.
- ✪ **ID-UL-ZUHA** – People kill a sheep to eat in memory of Abraham's willingness to sacrifice his son Isaac.

REPUBLIC DAY

Have you ever seen a National Day parade with elephants painted in bright colours? If you haven't, come to New Delhi on 26 January for Republic Day! While elephants and camels march down the street, aeroplanes put on an air show. There are people in all kinds of dress from the different regions of India. Dancers show off the dances of their region. What a show it is to see all these people come together to celebrate their country!

Come to the parade

On a low hill in the centre of New Delhi is a red sandstone palace where the president of India lives. Below is a grassy mall. This is where the Republic Day parade takes place. Long rows of wooden benches are set up. In the centre is an armchair under a gold umbrella. The president sits there to review the parade. Troops of horsemen ride past wearing red coats and gold turbans. Next come the elephants, their trunks painted with flowers. Soldiers and sailors, boy scouts and girl guides, and patriotic groups march past in their uniforms. Then come the floats representing the states of the Republic of India. Each is brightly decorated to show off the best of its state.

This elephant is decorated to march in the parade. National heroes have the honour of riding on the elephants.

A corps of women soldiers marches in perfect form.

What is Republic Day?

Indians have two independence days. Republic Day is the anniversary of the day in 1926 when Indians declared their independence from Great Britain. India also celebrates Independence Day, the day 20 years later when the British turned over power to Pandit Jawaharlal Nehru, India's first prime minister. On Independence Day, the president makes a speech. But the real show takes place on Republic Day, when the weather is cool and it is a nice time to sit outside and watch a parade.

The camel corps from the desert region of Bikaner is one of the highlights of the parade.

Independence

Many years ago, India was a colony of Great Britain, but Indians wanted to run their own country. They thought the British were using India to make themselves rich while Indians stayed very poor. People believed they had to force the British to leave. But the British were strong and the Indians had no army. What could they do?

A great man

Mohandas K. Gandhi was a leader of the Indian struggle for independence. People call him Mahatma Gandhi. *Mahatma* means "Great Soul". He believed that it was wrong to kill anyone. He thought the best way to make the British leave was to refuse to obey unfair laws. He called this "passive resistance".

Make your own salt

When the British put a tax on salt that made it very expensive for Indians, Gandhi announced he was going to make salt himself. He started walking to the sea, which was 240 kilometres away. As he walked, people joined him. Finally, there were thousands of people marching. When people saw this, they realised that the British couldn't tax them without their consent. After many demonstrations like this one, the British were forced to leave.

When he was young, Gandhi wore trousers and shirts, but later he wanted to be closer to the common people of India, so he started to dress like a simple farmer. He also learnt how to spin yarn and wore hand-woven clothes. People loved him because he shared the life of the simple people.

Dancers come from all parts of the country to represent their local area. Here, a troupe of Sikhs dances the bhangra in the parade. Sikh men never cut their hair and cover it with a turban as a mark of their religion. Guru Nanak started the Sikh religion to bring Hindus and Muslims together. He wanted to show people that God was neither Hindu nor Muslim, but included both.

Let's dance

After Republic Day comes a two-day festival of music and dance. India has its own forms of music and dance that go back thousands of years and are admired all over the world. *Baharat Nhatyam* and *Kathak* are two types of traditional dance. Kathak dancers wear bands with rows of bells on their ankles. They make a rhythm with the bells as they move.

India is famous for its beautiful **sitar** music. The **sitar** is a large stringed instrument that makes a sound very different from any other instrument. Ravi Shankar is a famous sitar player. With the sitar you are likely to hear the **tabla**, a kind of Indian drum. Zakir Hussain is a popular tabla player.

Indian dance was at first a way of worshipping the gods. Most dances tell a story about gods or heroes.

11

DIVALI

It's late autumn in India, and the long nights are dark as the moon comes to the end of its monthly cycle. On the last days of Ashwin (that's the Hindu month that falls in October or November), rows of small, flickering clay lamps appear in doorways, on windowsills, even lighting the outlines of towering government buildings. These are the lights of Divali, the Festival of Lights. Divali is dedicated to Lakshmi, the Hindu goddess of wealth and beauty. During the five days of Divali, Lakshmi visits houses and shops that are clean and well lit. And with her she brings wealth and good fortune, so all of India is lit up to invite her in.

A new beginning

To get ready for Divali, Indians buy new clothes and clean, and maybe paint, the house. Shopkeepers start a new year, and everyone pays off what they owe. Divali is a time to start afresh, with the hope that Lakshmi will bring better fortune in the next year. Hindus go to their temples to honour the gods. Then they come home and eat special meals. Later, they visit family and friends, bringing gifts of sweets. It is traditional to give sweets at Divali. Want to know how Divali started? Listen to a story . . .

A Hindu goddess is decorated for Divali. Hindu gods and goddesses often have several sets of arms to show how powerful they are.

Here are rows and rows of sweets, flowers and fruit laid out as offerings to the gods.

The Demon of Filth

Once there was a demon named Naraka. Naraka was very dirty, so he was called the Demon of Filth. He never took a bath or cleaned his house. He kidnapped young girls and took them to live in his dirty house. One of those girls was Lakshmi.

Krishna (one of the most popular Hindu gods) fought with Naraka and won. As Naraka was dying, he felt sorry that he had made people unhappy. He asked Krishna to make the anniversary of his death a day when people would be happy. That day is Divali. People celebrate by taking scented baths and dressing up in new clothes.

Divali lights on a street in Rajasthan.

13

The lights of goodness

Divali means "row of lights". On the long, dark nights of Divali, the lamps remind people that goodness and wisdom are stronger than the forces of darkness. There are many stories that people tell about Divali, but all of them are about the triumph of good over evil. Here's another story about the victory of good over evil that is part of the Divali tradition.

Lights invite Lakshmi to bring good fortune. A tradition for young girls is to set Divali lamps afloat in the river. If the light burns as long as its owner can see it, she will have good luck in the next year.

One of the stories that goes with Divali is that of the hero Rama's return to his kingdom. Here, people use dance to tell the story of Rama's adventures. These dance dramas are popular during Dussehra and Divali.

Here are statues of the evil Ravenna and his son and brother ready to be set on fire.

Rama comes home

Many Indian festivals celebrate several things at once. Divali lights also remind Hindus of the story of Rama's return to his kingdom. According to the story, Rama, an Indian hero, was unfairly sent away from his kingdom. Then, the demon Ravenna kidnapped Rama's wife. Rama spent years searching for her. Finally, there was a big battle, and Rama destroyed Ravenna. When Rama returned to his kingdom, the people lit lamps to guide him back.

During the holiday of Dussehra, which comes just before Divali, people put up giant statues of Ravenna. At the end of the festival, they put firecrackers inside the statues and set them on fire. Divali is when Rama returned to his kingdom. On that night, Indians light lamps to celebrate Rama's return.

Holi

If you're in India one day in March and someone comes up and throws red powder all over you, don't be surprised. This is Holi, and on Holi people walk around yelling "Holi hai, Holi hai" and throwing coloured water or powder at anyone they see, even if it's their teacher or the mayor of their town. During Holi, everyone is equal and everything is forgiven. The important things are "rang, ras and rag" (colour, dance and song). So get in on the fun, throw a little powder and join in the dancing and singing. This is the Festival of Colours. All the rules are off.

Some people use bicycle pumps to squirt red, yellow and green liquid over everyone.

A fun time

On the first night, the young men and boys make a huge bonfire. People have to watch closely around Holi or their fence might end up on the bonfire. Men and boys dance around the fire, sometimes jumping through it. Food that has just been harvested is put on the fire as an offering. The next morning, the fun begins. Besides the colour throwing, there are huge fairs and circuses. People forget whatever fights they have had with anyone. It's a time to start afresh.

Different coloured powders are offered for sale on the streets. These colours usually wash out of clothes without too much trouble. But I wouldn't wear my best clothes on Holi if I were you!

Beating up the boys

Near Delhi, the women of one village pretend to have a fight with the men of a nearby village. The women carry long bamboo poles. They try to hit the men with their poles. The men carry leather shields. They dodge through the crowds, trying to escape the women. When the women get tired, the men shout insults to get them started again. It's all for fun, and everyone has a good laugh.

Although Holi is a Hindu festival, it is a big carnival that people of all religions join in. A nice thing about Holi is the way it breaks down barriers.

In the evening, people change into clean clothes. They get together in public squares to eat, drink, talk and watch local folk dances.

The Holi story

There are many stories about Holi in different parts of the country. The best known is about a young prince named Prahlad. Prahlad worshipped the god Vishnu. He was very religious. His father wanted everyone to worship him. He was very angry that his son refused to obey him. He asked his evil daughter, Holika, to help him punish his son. Holika had the power to walk through fire without being burnt. She carried Prahlad into a bonfire. People heard terrible screams and thought that Prahlad was burning to death. Finally, Prahlad walked out alone. His faith had protected him while the evil Holika burnt. That's why there are bonfires for Holi today.

Think about this
Does your family spring clean? At one time, rubbish was taken out and burnt on bonfires during spring festivals. This was a way of getting rid of the remains of winter and starting afresh. In Britain, people still have a day of practical jokes once a year – do you know when it is? (Hint: It's close to the same time as Holi.)

Opposite: People also remember the god Krishna at Holi. This is a painting of Krishna as a cowherd. When he was a boy, he was very mischievous and was always playing pranks. He stole milk from the milkmaids. To get him back, they threw coloured powder over him. That is why people throw coloured powder at each other during Holi.

Celebrating springtime

Holi is also very much like many other spring festivals around the world. Many people celebrate the return of spring with bonfires and a noisy festival where people act wild and crazy. It is a time to be happy that winter is over and food is starting to grow again. In India, the spring wheat harvest comes around this time of year.

FOR THE BEASTS

Animals have an important place in Indian life, and Indians have great respect for them. There are several festivals in India that are for animals, to thank them for their help during the year. For Pooram, elephants wear gold head ornaments in a parade. The men riding on the elephants carry brightly coloured umbrellas and peacock feather whisks. Naag Panchami is the Festival of the Snakes. People give milk and flowers to snakes that live in the temples. A special event for camels is the Pushkar Mela.

Come to the fair

Melas, or village fairs, accompany many religious festivals in India. There are also special melas where people come to trade animals. People come to the fair from all around, dressed in their best clothes. Stalls sell everything you can imagine, from pots and pans to jewellery for women, fruit and vegetables, and cows and horses (or camels!). There are magic shows, street dances, puppet shows and circuses. No matter what their religion, everyone enjoys a mela!

A Rajasthani couple take a ride around the fair on their camel. People from Rajasthan wear traditional clothes different from those in other parts of India. Women often wear nose rings, like this woman.

The camels visit Pushkar

A camel shows off the tricks it is able to do.

Once a year, the little town of Pushkar in Rajasthan (find it on the map on page 5) comes alive with the biggest camel fair anywhere. People come from the deserts around Pushkar to trade camels and enjoy the fair. There are camel races and camel beauty contests and singing and dancing. Merchants sell everything a camel needs, like colourful saddles and embroidered cloth covers with little mirrors. In the evening, thousands of campfires light up the desert night, and the sounds of folk melodies fill the air.

On the night of the full moon, people take a dip in Pushkar Lake. The lake is sacred to Hindus.

21

Ponggal

Hindus believe cows are very special animals, so they don't kill them. In Tamil Nadu, a province in southern India, they have a festival where they honour the cows. It's called Ponggal, which is also the name of a sweet treat made from rice, milk and brown sugar. Part of the Ponggal Festival is to make ponggal treats and offer them to the gods. Ponggal celebrates the rice harvest, so they use the new rice they have just picked. After they offer it to the gods, everyone shares the treats. They also offer the gods clay statues of horses to thank them for sending rain for the growing rice.

Women take advantage of the holiday to look around the marketplace. They have their hair decorated with flower garlands for the festival.

For Ponggal, people like to decorate their front steps. This woman has come up with a lovely pattern using moistened rice flour.

Thanks to the cows

On the third day of Ponggal, it's time to thank the cows. The men and boys take the cows out and give them a good bath. Then they paint their horns. Blue and gold are favourite colours. They hang garlands of flowers around their necks and put bright feathers in their hair. Often, there are parades and music for the cows. They get to eat some of the ponggal, too.

Let's play tag

At the end of the day, people have bullfights. But they don't kill the bull like people do in some other countries. In India, they put a packet of money between the horns of the bull and garlands of money around its neck. Then men try to snatch the money away. Sometimes it can be dangerous for the men.

A cow is dressed in its festival best for Ponggal.

RAKSHA BANDHAN

There is no Mother's Day, or Father's Day, in India but there is a day for brothers and sisters. It is called Raksha Bandhan. On this day, sisters tie a bracelet called a *rakhi* around their brothers' wrists. The rakhi is supposed to protect the brother from anything bad that might happen in the next year. The sister also puts a dot of red powder on her brother's forehead and gives him treats. In return, the brother promises to care for his sister and gives her a present.

Special friends

Even after they've grown up, women give rakhi to their brothers and make them treats. In return, a man might give his sister a new sari. It is a way of saying that even if they fight sometimes, they will always care for each other. Sometimes, women "adopt" a brother for Raksha Bandhan. This could be a friend they feel especially close to. They then become "Rakhi brother" and "Rakhi sister".

A group of men show off the rakhi their sisters have given them. Often on Raksha Bandhan, young men spend the day parading around the streets, showing off their rakhi. It is a great honour to receive a rakhi since it shows that someone cares greatly for you.

Opposite: This little girl is tying a rakhi on her baby brother. In return, he gives her some fruit and money.

THINGS FOR YOU TO DO

If you were in India at festival time, you might want to play a game. How about *Pachisi?* Pachisi has been played in India for hundreds of years. Indians still enjoy a good game of Pachisi today. It takes two, three or four people. Each person will need some kind of playing piece, or token – either yellow, red, blue or green. You will also need a die that is white on two sides and yellow, red, blue and green on the other four sides. Use the playing board on the next page. The object is to move all the way around the board and then up the diagonal strip from your home square to the star in the centre.

How to play Pachisi

Put your marker in the corner of the board marked with your colour. Have someone throw the die until a colour comes up. The person with that colour begins. Throw the die. If it comes up the same colour as your marker, move one space counterclockwise and throw again. If it comes up white, don't move but throw again. If any other colour comes up, your turn is over. The person on your right is next. Play continues in this way. The first person to get to the centre wins.

Further information

www.bbc.co.uk/schools/religion/hinduism/diwali.shtml – information about the different religions of India and their festivals

www.hindunet.org/festivals/ – website with lots of information about all the Hindu festivals and customs

www.diwali.co.uk/ – website dedicated to the Hindu festival of Divali

www.indianmirror.com/festivals/festive.html – information about different festivals of India

Every effort has been made by the Publisher to ensure that these websites are suitable for children and contain no inappropriate or offensive material. However, because of the nature of the Internet, it is impossible to guarantee that the contents of these sites will not be altered. We strongly advise that Internet access is supervised by a responsible adult.

MAKE A DIVALI LAMP

You can make your own Divali lamp to light your house at Divali. Use the kind of clay that hardens by itself unless you know someone with a kiln who can fire it for you. Real Divali lamps are filled with oil. Then a wick is put in and lit. We use a candle to be safer.

You will need:
1. Air-hardening clay
2. Poster paint
3. Paintbrushes
4. Water
5. Tea light

1 Break off a handful of clay and roll it into a ball. Knead it well to make it soft enough to work with. Wet the clay from time to time as you work to keep it from drying out.

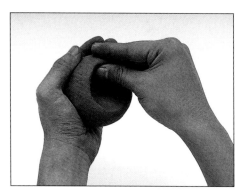

2 Mould the clay into either of the two lamp shapes shown below by hollowing out a well in the ball. Keep working the clay until the sides are the right thickness. Keep the clay thick around the edge to form a lip. Make the bottom flat so it will sit steady. When your lamp looks the way you want it, set it aside to dry.

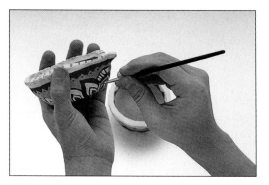

3 When your lamp has dried all the way through, it's time to paint it. Use strong colours to make it look nice and bright. You can put some designs on the inside, too. After the paint has dried, put a tea light inside and you're all done!

MAKE BURFI

Here is a simple kind of Indian treat. Try making burfi for Divali. There are many different kinds of burfi made with different kinds of nuts and flours. After you've tried your own, look for a shop that sells Indian snacks and sample some other kinds. You're sure to like them!

You will need:
1. 500 g raw cashews
2. Blender
3. 240 ml sweetened condensed milk
4. Butter
5. Pastry brush
6. 1 teaspoon flour
7. Measuring spoons
8. Small saucepan
9. Frying pan
10. Baking tray
11. Wooden spoon
12. Knife

1 Put the cashews in a frying pan and cook them over a low heat, stirring constantly, until they are golden brown. Be careful not to burn them!

2 Ask an adult to help you grind the roasted cashews. You can use a blender or crush them with a rolling pin.

3 Mix half the ground cashews, the condensed milk and the flour in a saucepan. Cook the mixture for a few minutes until it is almost solid.

4 Grease the baking tray with the butter. Press the cashew mixture into the greased pan. Pour the remaining cashews over the top and press them into the mixture. Let it cool and then cut into squares.

GLOSSARY

Baharat Nhatyam, 11	A traditional dance of India.
bhangra, 6	A folkdance performed by Sikh men at Baisakhi.
Caucasians, 4	White people who settled in India.
Dravidians, 4	Dark-skinned people who lived in India long ago.
Hindi, 3	The official language of northern India.
Kathak, 11	A traditional Indian dance using bells around the ankles.
lunar, 6	Following the phases of the moon.
mahatma, 10	A title of respect meaning "Great Soul".
mela, 3	A fair.
rakhi, 24	A bracelet given to brothers on Raksha Bandhan.
sitar, 11	An Indian stringed instrument with a long neck.
tabla, 11	A pair of drums of different sizes used in Indian music.
vegetarian, 23	Someone who eats no meat or fish.

INDEX